life in our hands

*For Marjorie
and Elizabeth*

The London Lectures in
Contemporary
Christianity

John Bryant & John Searle

life in our hands

a Christian perspective on genetics and cloning

Inter-Varsity Press

Inter-Varsity Press
38 De Montfort Street, Leicester LE1 7GP, England
Website: www.ivpbooks.com
Email: ivp@uccf.org.uk

First published 2004

British Library Cataloguing in Publication Data
A catalogue record for this book is available from the British Library.

ISBN 0–85111–795–3

Set in Adobe Garamond 11/12.5pt
Typeset by CRB Associates, Reepham, Norfolk
Printed by Creative Print and Design (Wales), Ebbw Vale

Inter-Varsity Press is the publishing division of the Universities and Colleges
Christian Fellowship (formerly the Inter-Varsity Fellowship), a student movement
linking Christian Unions in universities and colleges throughout Great Britain, and
a member movement of the International Fellowship of Evangelical Students. For
more information about local and national activities write to UCCF, 38 De
Montfort Street, Leicester LE1 7GP, email us at email@uccf.org.uk, or visit the
UCCF website at www.uccf.org.uk.

CONTENTS

PREFACE

The London Lectures in Contemporary Christianity were founded by John Stott in 1974 with the aim of informing Christians and helping them to engage with and think biblically about the issues of the day. In 2002 the London Lectures were given by John Bryant under the title *Moving Genes – Evolving Promise or Un-Natural Selection.* This book is based on those lectures, although some issues are discussed at greater depth in the book than was possible in the more conversational style – and within the time constraints – of the lectures.

In selecting genetics, genetic modification and cloning as the theme for 2002, the organizing committee of the London Lectures Trust had certainly identified some of the hot topics of the early twenty-first century. Advances in biological and biomedical science are raising many ethical and social issues, but the advances are occurring so quickly that they catch many people off guard. The ethical implications of one new finding or technique have barely been realized before the next dilemma arises.

Over the last fifteen years we have become increasingly engaged in discussing these dilemmas, through lecturing and writing, with different groups of people. We have taught on courses for under-graduates and postgraduates, as well as meeting professional groups, clergy and ministers in training. We have been particularly encour-aged by the increasing interest of Christians and church groups in the issues which scientific advances raise and by their willingness to think biblically when contributing to the debates.

One of the difficulties in addressing these issues is that for many of them the Bible does not contain precise guidance. A major part of our task, therefore, has been to discern the biblical principles which apply to these scientific developments. This is of course part of the long history of Christian engagement with society in seeking to draw out from Scripture what is God's way of living. It is in following that way that the health and welfare of society reside. However, we recognize that in the areas we discuss, as in many others, Christians who are equally committed to following the teaching of Scripture come to different conclusions. We have therefore tried to present these differing views while, where appropriate, making clear the conclusions we ourselves have come to. We have not sought to tell our readers what to think, but we hope that we have provided the tools to help them in their thinking.

We know from our own experience that people on all sides of these debates hold their views with deep conviction and sometimes express them with passion. It is our hope and prayer that this book will help our readers to appreciate and respect those views which may differ from their own. Our prayer is also that, as more is understood of God's amazing gifts to humankind through scientific developments, these may be used for the welfare of our fellow humans and the glory of his name.

In formulating our thinking we have benefited from discussions with many friends and colleagues, among whom also there is a range of views. We wish to thank particularly Linda Baggott la Velle, Caroline Berry, Celia Deane-Drummond, Steve Hughes, Suzi Leather, Joe Perry, Christopher Southgate, Philippa Taylor, Peter Turnpenny and also the members of the Evangelical Alliance working group on GM crops and food. John Bryant is grateful to the organizers of the London Lectures, especially Betty Baker and John Grayston, and we both very much appreciate the support and encouragement that John Stott has given us. We are also grateful to Stephanie Heald and Kate Byrom at IVP for their help in bringing the text to publication; we thank Stephanie for her patience when we encountered unforeseen delays in finishing the manuscript. Finally, we thank especially our wives, Marje and Elizabeth, for encouraging us to undertake this project and for their unfailing patience while we have brought it to fruition.

John Bryant
John Searle
Exeter, UK
July 2003

1. SETTING THE SCENE

Now we see but a poor reflection as in a mirror; then we shall see
face to face. Now I know in part; then shall I know fully...
(1 Cor. 13:12)

My uncle Bertram Twitt was a great man. He told me so himself.
One can't argue with facts like that.
(Spike Milligan)

The social climate

'May you live in interesting times.' This ancient Chinese curse clearly
regarded the quiet life, the status quo, as being infinitely preferable to
change, uncertainty or revolution. Today we certainly live in
interesting times, but we doubt whether many people feel cursed by
this. We may feel challenged, concerned and at times perplexed or
even worried, but certainly not accursed.

In the context of this book, the interest of the times lies in two
areas. The first is the rapid advance of biological science, with its
increasing power to manipulate the very stuff of life, to influence the
development of living organisms, to modify their patterns of genetic
inheritance and to make genetic copies of even complex animals.
Further, many of these technical advances are applicable to humans.
We are able to obtain detailed genetic knowledge about individuals
and the probability of their suffering from particular diseases; we can
test for genetic lesions at all stages of existence, from a few-celled
embryo created by *in vitro* fertilization to an adult. The technology is
available to change, albeit in a modest way, the genetic make-up of
future human beings and even to attempt cloning of humans. Most
of these advances are recent; the pace with which some areas of
biology are moving means that some of today's routine procedures,
such as determining the sequence of complete sets of genes, were
undreamed of thirty years ago – or if they were dreamed of, they
remained a gleam in the eye of the biological scientist.

For some, this acquisition of knowledge is worrying. Humans have power to manipulate life, including human life, and this power can be used for good or ill. The advance of biology, however, has been so rapid that it has run far ahead of the ethical debate. How extensively, for example, had the implications of human cloning been discussed outside the realm of fiction before the announcement in 1997 of the birth of Dolly? And it is clear not only that the advances in biology are running ahead of ethical thinking, but that they are also raising very new situations in which that thinking may be applied. Audrey Chapman writes of human society facing 'unprecedented choices' (Chapman, 1999). She urges Christians to become engaged with the issues and to participate in an informed manner in the debate. We agree wholeheartedly with this plea and have set out those issues later in this volume.

The second area of interest is the cultural climate in which these advances are taking place. The prevailing philosophy is postmodernism (see Cook, 1996). We discuss this more fully in the next section; here we need to note that one of its main thrusts is that concepts of truth are socially constructed. Truth therefore becomes local or even personal: there is no 'big story', or, in technical terms, no meta-narrative. It will be immediately obvious that there is no room in postmodernism for overarching religious beliefs or for absolute moral values. Furthermore, because it claims to be seeking verifiable truth about objective reality, science too is under threat.

The other relevant aspect of culture is that in the UK and in several other European countries our Christian consensus has been lost.[1] Obviously, postmodernism has no room for general truth such as is presented in Christianity; the decline in Christian belief may thus be partly ascribed to current philosophical trends, although this decline has been going on for over 200 years. However, many who do not espouse postmodernism nevertheless actively reject the possibility of religious truth. Thus the influential writer and genetic scientist (and definitely modernist) Richard Dawkins writes: 'Is there no catastrophe terrible enough to shake the faith of people . . . in God's goodness and power? No glimmering realization that he might not be there at all: that we might just be on our own, needing to cope with the real world

---

1. Readers in the USA may feel that in their country there is a Christian consensus, but it is difficult to determine whether that results from personal conviction or from a social adherence to traditional values.

like grown-ups?' (Dawkins, 2003: 160).[2] There is no doubt that views such as these are widely accepted.

How then did we come to be in this state? We will examine this under three headings:

- Modernism and postmodernism
- The nature and practice of science
- Science and belief

Modernism and postmodernism

In northern and western Europe, the expansion of scientific endeavour in the early seventeenth century is often taken as the beginning of modernism. There was confidence that science could uncover objective reality about the world, although it was recognized that, at any one time, knowledge of that reality is partial and provisional. There was no room for the idea that 'truths' about the world might be based in the culture or the person by whom that truth had been discovered. Further, many of the early modernists, including scientists, were theists (or at least deists) and acknowledged that they were investigating the work of God. There is clearly an underlying metanarrative, a big story, namely that God is creator and sustainer of the universe. However, acknowledgment of that metanarrative is not in fact necessary for the pursuit of science. What is needed is the confidence mentioned above: that there are objective truths concerning the world that do not alter from place to place or from culture to culture.

Thus there was a gap in the wall: belief in a creator God is not a prerequisite for investigating the world. So, by the middle years of the nineteenth century, the Christian consensus was weakening. Gwen Raverat in *Period Piece*, her lovely book about growing up in Cambridge in the second half of the nineteenth century, recalls the young people's realization that rejection of Christianity and even espousal of atheism were now socially acceptable. Nevertheless, the modernist agenda remained firmly in place and continued well into the twentieth century. However, the drift had started which

---

2. Based on an article in *The New Humanist*, Winter 2001, special 'After Manhattan' edition.

transferred the emphasis from the glory of God in creation to the glory of humankind in their ingenuity.

We now turn to postmodernism. This label is applied to a set of overlapping philosophies; thus there are different versions that emphasize different features within the overall trend. Here we have tried to present the 'essence' of the postmodern approach. Some writers trace the beginnings of postmodernism back to the eighteenth century and especially to the work of the philosopher Immanuel Kant (see Carson, 2002). In particular, it has been said that his argument that universal moral values – categorical imperatives, as he called them – could be derived by activity of the intellect meant that different intellects might come up with different values. Kant would have surely denied this, but perhaps the seed was sown. However, we are on much firmer ground in discussing the nineteenth-century philosopher Nietzsche (Robinson, 1999). Famously declaring that God is dead, he proposed that absence of any external reference points meant that each individual is his or her own arbiter of moral and cultural values. Ideas of truth and culture thus become very fragmented. There are two further elements here. First, if there are no universal values, is it not possible that the values I have accepted may be reworked; that the persona I have adopted may be changed? So, individuals may reinvent themselves. The singer and actor Madonna thus represents the ideal postmodern icon.[3]

Nietzsche, however, took his argument further than this. Since there is no God, each person can become his or her own god; ethical decision-making then becomes a matter of deciding which line of action has the best outcome – the best consequences for the individual. This is known as rational egoism, and it clearly turns on its head the idea that self-centredness is sinful. That is not to say that all admirers of Nietzsche or all postmodern thinkers have adopted rational egoism as their ethical framework, but it does highlight another key feature of postmodernism as it is now understood. If your world-view – your concept or version of the truth – is as valid as anyone else's, then your ethical value system is also as valid as anyone else's. Beliefs, values and morals are thus socially constructed, strongly influenced by culture and therefore not necessarily relevant or even tenable in other cultures.

---

3. We are grateful to Jock McGregor and David Cook for this example: see Cook 1996: 15–16.

If the roots of postmodernism go back to the nineteenth century, then its growth and flowering are very much of the twentieth and early twenty-first centuries. The philosopher Wittgenstein insisted that words, including scientific terms, must be interpreted in their social context. While it is clear that culture will certainly affect the perceived meanings of words, a problem arises if we assume that this means there can be no underlying universal truth. We certainly see the latter conclusion in the work of writers such as Derrida and Foucault and the 'deconstructionist' school of literary criticism, all of whom emphasized the absence of universal truths, of overriding themes or metanarratives. There is no doubt that these ideas have become thoroughly embedded (although far from universally held) in academic philosophy, sociology and the humanities, particularly since the 1970s. The Christian writer and broadcaster Elaine Storkey (whose early career years were in academic sociology) recently commented that, while it is now acceptable to assert in serious academic circles that 'all things are relative', such a statement would not have been widely tolerated prior to the widespread infiltration of postmodernism.[4] Thus, although we may identify relativism as a philosophy in its own right, it is clearly also embedded in post-modern thinking. Of course, the statement that 'all things are relative' cannot be sustained because it is actually self-defeating, as ably demonstrated by a number of writers (e.g. Cook, 1996; J. Taylor, 2002). Some postmodernists, however, would argue that this in itself is a symptom of the absence of any overriding truths or principles and indicates the futility of trying to derive any.

It is admittedly difficult to ascertain the extent to which the man or woman in the street is consciously aware of postmodernism, although most Westerners, particularly those aged under fifty-five, actually think in a postmodernist way. It is clear, however, that its influence hugely pervades the media, and some elements of it may be perceived in, for example, the rejection of the findings of scientific enquiries if they fail to support particular preconceived ideas. If all 'truth' is culturally constructed, that includes scientific truth. It is for such reasons that both academic and popular expressions of post-modernism have been perceived as a threat to science (see the next section). There has also been an obvious effect on general ethical

---

4. University of Exeter, Annual University Service, Exeter Cathedral, October 2002.

thinking: in many areas of moral decision-making it is a matter of personal choice (see Cook, 1996: 45), although there are some deeds that are almost universally regarded as wrong. The theologian Don Carson writes that one outworking of postmodernism is that it is difficult to convey the concept of sin (Carson, 2002). While people are willing to describe certain acts, such as the murder of a child, as evil, there is no general acceptance of more widespread human sin, and thus no need is seen for redemption.[5] This has clear implications for the way in which we bring the good news of Jesus to present generations.

In this section we have suggested that in postmodernism there is no room for overriding concepts, general truths or metanarratives. We also note that this has clear knock-on effects for religion, for ethics and for science, since ideas about truth are taken to be outworkings of culture, socially constructed, rather than there being general truths that transcend culture. We now turn to look specifically at science.

The nature and practice of science

This is not a book about the philosophy of science. Nevertheless, it is concerned with the applications of certain aspects of biological science and the ethical implications of those applications. Science is concerned with knowledge – knowledge about the universe in which we live – and uses a number of methods to accumulate this knowledge (see below). Obviously, at any one moment, the knowledge is partial (humans do not and cannot know everything) and provisional (present understanding may be modified by subsequent findings). For this reason many aspects of scientific 'knowledge' are referred to as theories or hypotheses. Nevertheless, scientists assume that there is an objective reality to which this partial and provisional knowledge relates.

We are generally told that science progresses by use of experiment, measurement or observation in order to obtain data, followed by

---

5. Carson suggests that the terrorist attacks on New York and Washington on 11 September 2001 may have done more to roll back the postmodernist tide in the USA than any philosopher or preacher, because words like wickedness, evil and wrongdoing had re-entered everyday speech. Whether he is right, time will tell.

analysis of those data and the formulation of hypotheses or theories that may be tested by further experiments, measurements or observations. Further, Popper maintained that the only 'real' hypotheses were those that could be falsified (i.e. those for which there is the possibility of being proved wrong). The current view among both the scientific community and some philosophers of science, however, is that science is actually rather more flexible than this stereotype (see the discussions by Polkinghorne, 1998: 14–16, and J. Taylor, 2002). For a start, the standard description leaves out serendipity (making significant discoveries by accident), intuition (in which an interpretative leap is made that goes beyond the strict limits of what the data tell us) and even guesswork. By all accounts, turning one half of their model upside down was a 'lucky' guess by Watson and Crick (the main discoverers of the structure of DNA) – or was it a piece of brilliant intuition? (In the famous two-stranded helix, the double helix, of DNA structure the two strands have opposite orientation – one is 'upside down' in respect of the other.) Further, it is now recognized that scientific hypotheses come in a variety of forms. Some are of a very generally applicable nature and are so well established that they are best regarded as paradigms: evolution comes into this category. Other hypotheses are very local in application, and may also be very tentative because of the scarcity of relevant data. Experiments are often carried out in order to ascertain whether there is evidence to support rather than to refute a hypothesis. Indeed, Popper's criterion of being capable of falsification is difficult to apply across the board. As Polkinghorne (1998: 14–15) points out, 'we have learned some things scientifically that we are never going to have to revise. Atoms have come to stay and so has the helical structure of DNA. Popper cannot account for this gain in knowledge.'

The final point we need to make about the practice of science is its ethical framework. We are here talking not about the ethics of doing certain types of science, such as experiments on animals, but about the ethics of science itself. For as long as science has been a formalized activity, scientists have presented their results to the wider world by publishing them. In this way the body of scientific knowledge grows, hypotheses are created and proved or disproved and each scientist is able to build on what others have done. In the twentieth century the publication process became highly structured, and the research journals published across the world number several thousand. Nevertheless, science publication still retains a commitment to an ethical framework without which science could not progress: the scientist does not publish false data, or discard data that are inconvenient for his or her pet hypothesis. In other words, when presenting data the scientist is expected to tell the truth. Indeed, there are strict penalties for failing to do so. In one of C. P. Snow's early novels, *The Search*, the main character was denied the headship of a prestigious laboratory because, unbeknown to him, his research assistant had made up some data that had been published in a leading journal. In real life, in the late 1990s, a senior biological scientist in a major European laboratory was forced to resign when it was discovered that his research assistant had made up data that had been published in prestigious journals. And in 2002 a brilliant but ambitious young physicist was both denied an appointment to a senior position in a leading laboratory and dismissed from the post he was actually in because he had made up data that formed the basis of several major papers. Lying about data is thus regarded very seriously; rightly so, because in order for science to progress one must be able to trust what has gone before. This facet of the practice of science has clear implications in the GM debate, in which scientists are becoming accustomed to being called liars. We discuss this in Chapter 5.

We now focus on the relationship between scientific truth and postmodernism. While postmodernists may be happy to accept that scientists publish data they believe to be true, they will deny that the data have anything to do with objective reality. Indeed, postmodernism often presents general objective reality as fictional and its apparent manifestations as socially constructed. At its most extreme, as when expressed by the Edinburgh group known as the 'Strong Programme' (see J. Taylor, 2002), the suggestion is that the actual findings of science, the data collected, are socially constructed.

In response to that, we are happy to accept that scientists are not automata. Those who work in laboratories are whole people: people with personalities, with hopes, fears, prejudices, convictions; these features of who they are will affect the work they choose to do, the type of research they become involved in and so on. As Polkinghorne (1998: 15) points out, basing his comments on the views of the philosopher Michael Polanyi, 'The scientific method cannot be reduced to a well-formulated protocol whose execution could be delegated to a computer.' The pursuit of science 'is an activity of persons'. Thus, Francis Crick stated that he moved from physics into biology because he wished to dispel the last traces of vitalism[6] from the latter science. Further, there is a strong societal element in the support of science: some areas are deemed more worthy of support by public money or by commercial organizations. But none of this means that the results of scientific investigation are socially constructed. To quote John Taylor (2002), 'factors such as who is providing research funding do not *determine the outcome* of the research – although they will be involved in determining the topics that are chosen for research' (his italics).

Science is therefore totally at odds with postmodernism. Science works on the principle that there is an objective reality to be investigated. It recognizes that knowledge about and understanding of that reality is partial or provisional but that, as Carson (2002) points out so clearly, this does not mean that objective reality does not exist. Science is thus a thoroughly modernist activity. How, then, does it relate to Christian belief?

Science and belief

In the previous sections, we have shown that postmodernism denies the possibility of any kind of general, overriding truth and that this is clearly at odds with both Christianity and science. In that sense, Christianity and science are both facing the postmodern tide. This idea is further developed in Kirsten Birkett's useful little book *Un-natural Enemies* (Birkett, 1997), in which one of the arguments is that Christianity and science are allies in their rejection of post-modernism. However, the idea that Christianity and science may be 'on the same side' is one that will be foreign to many people (although probably not to most readers of this book). We need therefore to explore these ideas a little further.

Science has limits. Its role is to investigate physical reality, ranging from the smallest subatomic particle to the vastness of the universe, from the functioning of genes to the complex interactions of eco-systems. This does not mean, however, that no other forms of reality exist. That is the materialist fallacy: that the only reality is that which is open to investigation by the methods of science. There is nothing

---

6. An old idea that living things possess a special 'vital force' that cannot be explained in terms of their constituent parts.

in science itself that leads to this conclusion; indeed, we regard it as unscientific to close the mind to the possibility of other levels or forms of reality. The methods of science cannot directly investigate the spiritual world – it is outside the limits of science – but that does not negate the existence of that world. Thus, when a materialist such as Peter Atkins claims that science has made belief in God untenable, or when Richard Dawkins claims that science has shown that religion is outdated or even childish superstition, both are actually stepping outside the arena in which science has authority to speak. They reflect a trend that we mentioned under 'Modernism and postmodernism': that modernism has moved away from glorifying God to glorifying the works of humankind.

We thus argue that science and religious belief are entirely compatible. Space does not permit an extensive development of this theme, but for readers who are interested in following it up we can recommend the excellent texts by John Polkinghorne (*Science and Theology: An Introduction*, 1998), Roger Forster and Paul Marston (*Reason, Science and Faith*, 1999) and Denis Alexander (*Rebuilding the Matrix*, 2001). Here we want to return to the point made at the beginning of this section: that both science and Christianity acknowledge the existence of truths and realities that transcend culture. Of course, in Christian faith, as in science, such knowledge is very incomplete and in this earthly life will remain so: 'Now I know in part; then I shall know fully, even as I am fully known' (1 Cor. 13:12b). We must again emphasize, with Don Carson (2002), that incomplete knowledge of reality or incomplete understanding of objective truth does not negate the existence of that reality or truth. In the current postmodern climate David Cook urges us, 'Don't be defensive' (Cook, 1996: 3). Let us then be confident in the gospel of Christ and with that confidence endeavour, with the help of the Holy Spirit, to live out that gospel in our culture. This will surely mean, for some Christians at least, that we should tackle the key issues of the day. Some of those issues, those relating especially to genetics and allied topics, are set out in the rest of this book, starting, in the next chapter, with a consideration of ethical and bioethical decision-making within our current culture.

2. ETHICS AND BIOETHICS

I gain understanding from your precepts;
  therefore I hate every wrong path.
Your word is a lamp to my feet
  and a light for my path.
(Ps. 119:104–105)

If only God would send me a clear sign – like a numbered account
in a Swiss bank.
(Woody Allen)

What do we mean by ethics?

Ethics is about the values which people cultivate and the virtues they
exhibit. It is about what is right and what is wrong. It addresses the
question, 'What are our duties and responsibilities?' Jenny Teichman,
in her book *Social Ethics* (Teichman, 1996: 3), puts it like this:

> Ethics or moral philosophy aims to explain the nature of good
> and evil. It is important because whether we like it or not the
> human world is dominated by ideas about what is right and
> wrong, good and bad. Most ordinary conversations consist of
> value judgements. Every day, millions of people gossip about the
> awful things their neighbours have done or are suspected of
> having done. Every day, people pass judgement on politicians
> and other public figures.

Every day, people make decisions about what they ought or ought
not to do. Every time drivers enter a speed-limit zone they must
decide whether or not to keep to the limit. Somebody else has
already decided that the speed limit is necessary and what that
limit should be. Bioethics is an extension of this process into
biological and biomedical science. It discusses how we should use
modern biological and medical discoveries and technologies. The

fundamental questions are the same: is it right to do this or that? The decisions appear awesome, because of the ability of scientists to manipulate the basic biological material of human beings – the genes and cells – and thus influence what many regard as the very essence of human life.

Bioethics as a specific discipline developed during the second half of the twentieth century (see Bryant and Baggott la Velle, 2003). Its origins lie in two different areas of ethical thought. The first is environmental, following a succession of writers from Leopold in the 1940s via Carson and White in the 1960s to Van Rensselaer Potter in the 1970s. Leopold, as exemplified in his book *A Sand County Almanac* (1949), celebrated wilderness and was concerned about humankind's encroachment on the earth's wild places. Rachel Carson, in her seminal volume *Silent Spring* (1962), drew attention to the widespread pollution caused by profligate use and/or irresponsible disposal of certain agricultural and industrial chemicals. The title of the book alludes to the decline in songbird populations in parts of the USA because of accumulation of poisonous chemicals in the food chain. White (1967) blamed what he called the 'ecologic crisis' on anthropocentrism: the tendency of humankind to regard nature as existing for its own use. Potter brought these various themes together and coined the term 'bioethics' in his book *Bioethics: Bridge to the Future* (1971). Although Potter was a cell biologist whose professional life was spent in cancer research laboratories, he had a keen awareness of what human activity was doing to the natural world. He therefore suggested that in order to deal with human impact on the biosphere we needed to develop an ethical system that dealt not only with issues in human society and human-to-human interactions, but with the whole of the biosphere. Thus he saw 'bioethics as a bridge between the sciences and the humanities in the service of world-wide human health, and a protected environment'. The import of this has more recently been spelled out by Reiss (2002), who considers it appropriate to incorporate both trans-generational (having regard for subsequent generations) and trans-specific (having regard for non-human species of living organism) issues into bioethical thinking.

The second area of ethical thought is that of medical ethics: Jonsen (1998) argues that the medical strand within bioethics can be traced back to the Nuremberg trials in 1947. One outcome of the revelations about the atrocities committed during the Nazi regime was an initiation of critical examination of the professional activities of lawyers, scientists and medical practitioners (including those involved in medical research). This, Jonsen suggests, may be regarded as the birth of bioethics, or at least one major aspect thereof.

Both in bioethics and in more general areas of moral philosophy, religion is intimately bound up with decisions about what we ought and ought not to do. As Mary Warnock (1998: 7) puts it, 'though ethics, like the rest of philosophy, has been secularised, it is almost impossible to think about the origins and development of morality itself without thinking about its interconnection with religion'. Until recently, the Western world had largely forgotten this. Talking specifically about the major influence of Christianity on Western ethical thought, Warnock (1998: 79) writes, in a some-what understated way, that 'this ... does not prevent its sometimes being overlooked in the history of moral philosophy'. But since the atrocities committed in the name of Islam in the USA on 11 September 2001 ('9/11'), we have once again become acutely aware that religion is a powerful determinant of human behaviour. These events have also shown that it is not religion itself which drives some human conduct; it is the interpretation of religion which is crucial. For example, Muslims differ over whether Islam promotes or abhors acts of terror such as '9/11', and there is disagreement among Christians as to whether it is ever right to go to war.

For Christians, this link between what we believe and how we behave is central to our faith. Indeed, the evidence of genuine faith in Christ is a Christlike life. Jesus himself said that the evidence of discipleship was the love Christians had for each other (John 13:35). The apostle Paul challenged the Christians at Corinth about their sexual immorality, asking them, 'Do you not know that your body is the temple of the Holy Spirit?' (1 Cor. 6:19). Christians are not to conform to the culture in which they live; rather, the Holy Spirit is to transform their thinking and therefore their living (Rom. 12:2). Furthermore, this is not merely a matter of personal conduct. Christians are to influence the society in which they live. Jesus made it clear that his followers are to be salt and light in the world (Matt. 5:13–16). On the one hand they are to prevent society from going bad; on the other, they must be a positive force for good.

Ethical decision-making in contemporary society

Until perhaps the middle of the twentieth century, although a majority of the population was only nominally Christian, Christian values undergirded Western society. Thus, for example, the Ten Commandments were fundamental, at least in the criminal and civil law and in codes of public conduct. But at the beginning of the twenty-first century ethical decision-making has become very complex, because the society in which we live is:

- *Post-Christian.* Christian values are not the norm, even though Judaeo-Christian values remain as the foundation of our legal system.
- *Postmodern.* Truth, be it scientific or religious, is primarily a matter of personal preference, rather than being true either because God has revealed it or because science has demonstrated it. (See Chapter 1.)
- *Pluralist.* There are many different religious and philosophical systems, which vie with one another for people's allegiance. Many people decline to commit themselves to any particular system, but pick from different ones what appeals to them and reject what does not. Religion has become for some the spiritual version of the 'pick and mix' counter in a sweet-shop.
- *Complex.* Many of the issues about which decisions have to be made were completely unknown until two or three decades ago. The biblical writers did not know about them and it is therefore difficult to find detailed guidance in the Scriptures when making decisions about them.
- *Pragmatic.* The main question in decision-making is not 'Is this right or wrong?' but 'Will it work?'

Classically, ethical theories fall into two broad groups. *Deontological* ethics (Gk. *deon*, 'duty') is concerned with absolutes. Decisions are either right or wrong. Decision-making based on religious belief is often deontological: for example, being based on what are regarded as absolutist precepts, such as the Ten Commandments. *Consequentialist* ethics asks, 'What is the outcome of a particular decision? What benefit will be conferred or what harm will be caused?' These groups are of course subdivided and are the subject of detailed study in standard texts on ethics; for a succinct discussion see Draper 1994.

Here we need simply to point out that one version of consequentialism – utilitarianism (developed by Bentham and by Mill) – seeks consequences that bring the maximum pleasure or happiness or satisfaction. This is often regarded as having been developed as a counter to a more negative religion-based deontology, indicating among its proponents a highly stereotypical view of the general stance of Christian ethics.

However, both deontological and consequentialist systems have their limitations, and a third general approach based on *virtue* has been recognized (Rorty, 1979; MacIntyre, 1981). MacIntyre in particular emphasized the inadequacies of classical theories of moral discourse in dealing with the hard cases that are presented to us in modern life, such as abortion, and suggested that moral decision-making should seek the most virtuous outcome (see commentary by Moreno, 1991). There are problems with this approach, too, because one's view of what constitutes the higher virtues or of what is regarded as the most virtuous outcome is likely to depend on one's world-view. There is certainly extensive reference to virtue, ranging from wisdom to the fruit of the Spirit, in both the Old and New Testaments. A virtue approach to Christian behaviour was developed by the early church and by subsequent generations of Christian thinkers and writers, among whom we may mention St Thomas Aquinas as being especially influential. In connection with bioethics the approach based on virtue, or wisdom, has been extensively and eloquently developed by Deane-Drummond (2000, 2001, 2003).

In contemporary society there is little or no consensus about deontological decision-making. Very few ethical absolutes or duties are recognized. In public policy-making the primary mode of decision-making is consequentialist and utilitarian: that is, looking for the most benefit for the greatest number. The benefit–harm approach has been the key component in medical decision-making for generations. Doctors ask, 'What are the benefits of this particular treatment? What are the side effects?' If the balance is in favour of benefit, then the patient is advised to have the treatment or operation. This, of course, raises the question of what constitutes benefit. Chemotherapy in advanced cancer may confer the 'benefit' of six months' more life. But is that a 'benefit', if the quality of life during those six months is very poor?

For most people, decisions are usually determined by several factors. We may ask whether a particular course of action is reasonable. For example, if the continuation of a pregnancy to delivery presents a serious threat to the life of the mother, we may conclude that it is reasonable to terminate the pregnancy (see also Chapter 6). That decision involves the judgment that we place more value on the life of the mother than on that of the unborn baby. The difficulty with reason is that it is conditioned by our culture and by our natural inclination to pursue self-interest. Indeed, the atheist philosopher Nietzsche suggested that pursuit of self-interest was the only rational way to behave in a world where, according to his philosophy, there are no external moral reference points. This is reflected in current abortion practice in much of the Western world, where the grounds for terminating a pregnancy are often simply that the mother does not want to have the baby. For many people, that is reasonable (see also Chapter 6).

Feelings are another potent force in human behaviour. The media have a particularly powerful influence here. Television viewers see on their screens pictures of starving children in a famine-stricken area of Africa and are, quite properly, moved to make a credit-card donation to a relief agency. It is unlikely, however, that such a surge of feelings will move them to change their shopping habits so as to promote fair trade with the developing world, or to vote for increased taxation in order to increase aid.

Scientific developments may provoke a similar response of 'gut feeling'. On the one hand, this may be 'Yuk!': I feel that this is wrong, principally because it causes repugnance. In the late 1960s this was precisely the response of many people when Dr Christian Barnard performed the first heart transplant, and it has been an initial reaction to many of the techniques and developments we discuss here. On the other hand, the response may be 'Wow – this is terrific!': for example, to a medical advance that is (over-enthusiastically) claimed to have the potential to relieve widespread suffering. Some developments may elicit 'yuk' responses in some people and 'wow' responses in others, as happened when the birth of Dolly, the cloned sheep, was announced.

Where then do feelings and emotions fit into ethical decision-making? Human beings are whole people and emotions are part of that wholeness; they cannot be denied. Further, reactions based on emotions or feelings, whether 'yuk' or 'wow', may have at least a partial basis in deeply held cultural or religious values (see Midgley, 2000). However, we hold that emotional responses cannot be the *sole* arbiter in making decisions in bioethics. If they were, many biomedical advances would have been stopped in their tracks.

The third factor which people take into account is that of 'rights'. Autonomy and rights-based ethics have become a dominant factor in decision-making. Thus an infertile couple have a 'right to have a child'. A woman with an unwanted pregnancy has a 'right to an abortion'. A person dying from motor neurone disease has a 'right to euthanasia'. When a doctor makes a mistake the patient has a 'right to compensation'. Clearly, human beings do have rights: history is littered with examples where people have been denied their rights. But where there are rights without responsibilities and freedoms without duties, self-interest prevails, as both David Cook (2002) and Mary Warnock (1998) have pointed out so clearly. Indeed, Warnock is a strong critic of rights-based ethics, because in her view it can so easily lead to a weakening of our concepts of right and wrong (Warnock, 1998: 63); she is convinced 'that there cannot be a morality *founded* on the concept of rights' (Warnock, 1998: 71; her italics).

In 1989, two distinguished North American scholars expounded the principles of what they called 'biomedical ethics' in what became a seminal text in the field. They put forward guidelines for bioethical decision-making based on four principles (Beauchamp and Childress, 1979). Although they applied the guidelines particularly to medicine, they have a wide application. In summary, a doctor has four main ethical duties. The first is that of autonomy: that is to say, a person's rights and wishes must be respected. A doctor may not embark on a medical intervention against the wishes of a competent individual. Secondly, a doctor must not cause or inflict harm: the principle of non-maleficence. Thirdly, medical practice must observe the principle of beneficence: a doctor's duty is to do good, to bring about benefit. But, finally, a doctor has also to abide by the principle of justice. There are different approaches to justice in ethical theory, but there is an obligation on medical practitioners to look beyond the individual patient to the wider context and the resources in which they practise. These guidelines form a matrix which, although it does not always give clear answers to difficult ethical decisions, does provide a disciplined framework within which to think, so that the principles of deontology, utility and virtue are all considered. This approach has been criticized as a pallid, secular version of ethics. But the fact remains that in real life difficult decisions sometimes have to be made. Many doctors, including one of the authors of this book, have found it a great help in making such decisions about instituting or withholding complex medical treatments. The matrix approach, in our view, may be appropriately modified to provide a useful framework for making decisions in other areas: for example, animal welfare in agriculture.

So far, we have seen that contemporary ethical decision-making is not straightforward because:

- Scientific developments present us with previously undreamed-of possibilities.
- The issues raised by these developments are complex.
- There is no consensus about right and wrong.
- Utilitarian and rights-based philosophies dominate contemporary ethical thinking.

Christian ethical decision-making

Where does all this leave Christians, who not only have to make decisions about their own lives but are, on Jesus' instructions, to be 'salt' and 'light' in society (Matt. 5:13–16)? We inevitably turn to the Scriptures, which not only instruct us for salvation through faith in Jesus Christ but are also 'useful for teaching, for reproof, for correction and for training in righteousness' (2 Tim. 3:15–16, NRSV). It is from the Scriptures that we get understanding: they are a lamp to our feet and a light to our path (Ps. 119:105). To follow Jesus Christ is to accept him as our teacher and Lord. The evidence of our love for him is that we obey his commands (John 13:13; 15:10). However, what does this mean in relation to the possibilities which scientific developments open up and where the issues raised were unknown to the biblical writers? This raises three questions:

- What are the Scriptures?
- How do we interpret them?
- How do we apply them?

There is a huge literature about these questions; readers are referred to recent texts (Packer, 1993; McGrath, 1993; McGrath and Wenham, 1993). It is not part of our purpose to contribute directly to current debates, particularly within evangelicalism. Our approach to the use of the Scriptures in our understanding of the complex issues addressed in this book can be summarized as follows.

Scripture is God's revelation of himself to men and women. The *Scriptures* are the word of God communicated through the words of human beings, in a wide variety of literature: history, story, law, poems, songs, letters, narratives. Those who wrote them were inspired by God's Spirit. The people of God receive illumination from the same Spirit as they come to the Scriptures, humbly, prayerfully, to learn from him. The revelation of God centres on the person of the Lord Jesus Christ, whom the Bible describes as the living Word. It is through the written word of the Scriptures that we come to know the living Word, who is Jesus.

It is in this sense that the Scriptures are authoritative, since it is only those beliefs and practices which can be shown to be founded firmly in the Scriptures that Christians are required to follow. Article 6 of the Thirty-Nine Articles of the Church of England puts it like this:

> Holy Scripture containeth all things necessary to salvation: so that whatsoever is not read therein, nor may be proved thereby, is not to be required of any man, that it should be believed as an article of the Faith, or be thought requisite or necessary to salvation.

This is reflected in one of the questions which the bishop puts to those who stand before him requesting admission to the ordained ministry of that church: 'Will you be diligent in prayer, in reading Holy Scripture, and in all studies that will deepen your faith and fit you to uphold the truth of the Gospel against error?'

The process of *interpretation* seeks to clarify these beliefs and practices so that Christians may understand them and live by them. The principles of biblical interpretation are well known and can be summarized by the questions to be asked in studying a passage of Scripture. What sort of literature is it? Is it a carefully researched account, with particular themes and emphases within it, like Luke's Gospel? Is it the deepest expression of human longings or despair, as are some of the Psalms? Is it a story to address complex questions, like the book of Job? Is it a carefully argued theological treatise, such as the letter to the Romans? What is the historical and cultural context in which it was written? What is the central point the writer is making or the theme that is being pursued? What is the surrounding context of the chapter and the book? How does the text fit in with the overall teaching of the Bible? What do the words mean and how are they used?

This process requires us to use our minds: to think through what the text means and, where that is difficult, to work hard at it. We may have to examine the text in relation to present scientific understanding. We also read the Bible in the context of the long history of the church. Many before us have sought to interpret it and understand it. It is the corporate mind of the church, both past and present, which is a constraint against unbridled individualism in deciding what the Bible says. This is not to say that the Bible can be understood only by those with the appropriate academic training; God speaks through it to all those who come to it wanting to discern his will and do it. But it is a mistake (often with serious consequences for both individuals and churches) to use 'proof' texts to support a particular belief or practice.

For example, some Christians use the commandment 'Thou shalt not kill' to oppose abortion under any circumstances, or to support pacifism. In respect of the first, the command itself has nothing to do with abortion (the Bible contains no texts on abortion). In respect of the second, the people to whom the verse was addressed, the people of Israel, actually believed it was God's will to kill their enemies, even to the extent of 'ethnic cleansing'. Hays (1996: 1), puts it like this:

> 'The Devil can cite Scripture to his purpose,' so my grandmother used to say. Or, as we prefer to say now in the academy, 'The text has inexhaustible hermeneutical potential.' No matter how we choose to phrase it, the problem is the same. Despite the time-honoured Christian claim that Scripture is the foundation of the church's faith and practice, appeals to Scripture are suspect for at least two reasons: the Bible itself contains diverse points of view, and diverse interpretive methods can yield diverse readings of any given text.

Hays goes on to illustrate this from the differing responses in America at the beginning of the 1991 Gulf War. Billy Graham went to the White House to pray with President George Bush Sr as he launched Operation Desert Storm. Hours earlier, outside the White House, the presiding bishop of Bush's own denomination had joined a candlelight vigil praying for peace rather than for success in war.

Hays asks, 'Which group of Christians, those inside the White House or those outside the fence, had rightly discerned the Word of God?'

Rather than quoting proof texts, we have to come humbly to God's word praying that he will teach us his way, while recognizing gently and patiently that others equally committed to its authority may come to a different conclusion from the one we reach.

An important issue which has to be faced is the huge cultural gap between the world of the Bible and the world of the twenty-first century. The Bible was compiled by many writers and editors over a period of about 1,000 years and was completed 2,000 years ago. Those who wrote it and those who read it do so from within their respective cultures. This problem has been most helpfully addressed by John Stott through what he calls 'transposing the word' (Stott, 1992). The task, as he sees it, is to separate out the essence of God's revelation from its cultural clothing and then to reclothe it so that it can speak to contemporary culture. Stott gives as an example Jesus' command to his disciples to love one another. Here is an unequivocal obligation which he places on his followers. However, his demonstration of what this means by washing his disciples' feet is hardly applicable in a society using shoes and tarmacked roads. What is incumbent on us is to express our love for one another in humble, self-effacing service.

As we shall see later, this is an important principle in trying to make ethical decisions on the application of modern biomedical developments. For example, Jesus taught his followers not only to love one another but also to love their neighbours as themselves (Mark 12:31). The outworking of that in his own life and teaching, foreshadowed in the Old Testament and expounded in the New Testament letters, is that we should always put the welfare of others before our own. We are to treat others as more important than ourselves and to look to their interests (Phil. 2:3–4). In our view this principle is clearly contravened when individuals wish to perpetuate themselves (an erroneous notion anyway) by cloning, or when parents want a 'designer' baby to meet their own aspirations and requirements.

However, we still face many present realities and future possibilities which were not known to the biblical writers. In a very different field, where in Scripture is there specific guidance that would have helped in making decisions about how to treat the conjoined twins 'Jodie' and 'Mary', born in 2000? The dilemma which faced their parents, the doctors looking after them and the judges who had to decide what might lawfully be done was that not to separate them by a surgical operation would result in the death of both children, but to separate them meant that one could live and the other would die.[1] The court's judgment allowing them to be separated was, in our view, a model of clear, compassionate and principled decision-making using the principles of non-maleficence and beneficence with a strong virtue- or wisdom-based approach. There is a hint also of utilitarianism: namely, that one life is better than no life.

It is helpful to remember the biblical framework within which God works and human beings live: creation, fall, redemption and glory. God made human beings in his own image and likeness (Gen. 1:26–27, and see Chapter 3). God confers upon humankind certain responsibilities for its own well-being and makes certain prohibitions which, when transgressed, result in harm. This is the core of Genesis chapters 1 and 2. Men and women did, however, transgress those limits. There followed a breakdown in relationships with God, with each other and with the environment (Gen. 3). The next eight chapters of Genesis unfold the consequences of this disobedience to God.

Then there begins the story of God's rescue operation, culminating in the birth, life, death and resurrection of Jesus, whereby we may be forgiven, find new life and be gradually transformed by the Holy Spirit towards that divine image which was God's original intention. That process will one day be complete when those who follow Jesus will be like him, for they will see him as he is (1 John 3:2). Indeed, the whole creation will be transformed into what the last book of the Bible refers to as a new heaven and a new earth (Rev. 21:1–8). So the circle will be complete. That which God made perfect, but which men and women marred, is restored to perfection in a renewed cosmos.

We live in a fallen world and, therefore, scientific developments have the potential for both good and evil. Humankind has indeed a long and inglorious history of misusing God's good gifts. Wrongdoing may arise from deliberate action, by accident, or because a given action has the potential for either good or bad. Thus, cars can move people from one place to another safely and quickly. Yet drivers may kill a person *en route*, either because they drive dangerously or

---

1. *The Times*, 23 September 2000: 7.

carelessly or because the person may fail to see the car coming and so step off the pavement in front of it. Further, the very use of the car makes statements about the way we utilize the earth's resources, and there are some who oppose private transport on environmental ethical grounds.

There are many genetic technologies that have the potential for both good and wrongdoing. For example, GM technology could potentially be misused; there may be risks involved in gene therapy or GM crops; and there are ethical disagreements about the diagnostic prevention of genetic disease prior to implantation when this leads to the discarding of some embryos. The question, in all these areas, is whether concerns about potential for wrongdoing should prevent us from developing the technology further, or whether we can success-fully regulate the technology in order to prevent the problems arising (or at least to lessen significantly the potential for their arising).

Secondly, Christians will always try to make decisions that are compatible with their life within Christ's kingdom. Yet they also recognize that those decisions may be imperfect, even provisional, because the world in which they function is imperfect, their own transformation into Christlikeness is not complete, and the dawn of God's new earth and heavens is not yet. They may be able to achieve only decisions which are 'good enough'.

As we have grappled with the issues of this book over many years, we have sought wisdom,[2] trusting God to give it to us (Jas. 1:5) and praying, in the words of the Prayer Book Collect for Whitsunday, that we may 'have a right judgement in all things'. In making decisions we have found it helpful to work through the following ten-step process:

1. Collect the facts as currently known.
2. Evaluate the facts. How good is the evidence on which they are based? Is more evidence needed? Do the facts point to a different conclusion?
3. As far as is possible, interpret the facts.
4. Consult important sources: the Scriptures, the mind of the church (both past, where relevant, and present, as it considers the issue) and wise and informed people.

---

2. Celia Deane-Drummond suggests that divine wisdom in all its ramifications is the highest virtue we can seek.

5. Identify the key principles.
6. Put the principles in order of priority.
7. List the options.
8. Discuss them with others.
9. Pray: alone and/or with others.
10. Make a decision.

Remember that the decision may have to be reviewed.

This is not an easy process. Its value is that it imposes a discipline on decision-making. As pointed out before, it is all too easy to respond with 'Yuk!' or 'Wow!'; to apply biblical texts inappropriately; to allow one ethical theory to override others; or to be lazy or sink into despair, saying, 'This is too difficult.' We also recognize that different people will come to different conclusions and therefore different actions. Christians often find this particularly difficult to accept, but here, as in so many disputes within the church, the famous epigram (usually attributed to Augustine of Hippo, but in fact originating from the seventeenth-century Lutheran scholar Robertus Meldinius) surely applies: 'In essentials, unity; in non-essentials, liberty; in all things, charity.'

3. MADE IN THE IMAGE OF GOD

I am fearfully and wonderfully made.
(Ps. 139:14)

The universe we observe has precisely the properties we should expect if there is, at bottom, no design, no purpose, no evil, no good, nothing but blind pitiless indifference ... DNA neither cares nor knows. DNA just is. And we dance to its music.
(Richard Dawkins)[1]

Introduction

Many people in the Western world will always remember precisely where they were and what they were doing on 11 September 2001, as first one and then a second aircraft were flown deliberately into the Twin Towers of the World Trade Center in Manhattan, New York. The British prime minister, Tony Blair, was about to address the annual conference of the Trades Union Congress. He did not deliver his prepared speech, but instead made an immediate response to what had happened, during which he said: 'These people [terrorists] have no respect for the sanctity of human life.' He thereby gave succinct expression to a deep human instinct that human life is special.

Later that same year, on 29 November, George Harrison, one of the three remaining Beatles, died. In his earlier years he had underplayed the fame, glamour and wealth of their success. He was probably the most thoughtful member of the group; it was he who persuaded the others to visit India to seek spiritual enlightenment. In later life he retained an awareness of the spiritual dimension: he often said that the search for God cannot wait, and continued as an adherent of the Hare Krishna movement[2] that had so interested him

---

1. From Dawkins (1995), *River out of Eden*, p. 155.
2. Essentially, a branch of Hinduism in which Krishna is elevated to supreme status over the other Hindu gods.

in younger days.[3] He also emphasized the importance of seeking answers to the basic questions about human life. Who am I? Why am I here? Where am I going? What is intrinsically special about George Harrison when the achievements, the money and the celebrity status have all been stripped away?

What are human beings? A biological perspective

Harrison's first question – 'Who or what am I?' – has been brought into sharp relief by the discoveries of modern molecular biology. As the human genetic map has been unrolled the questions have been increasingly asked. Are we only what our genes make us? What else influences who we are and what we are like? Do we have free will? The distinguished Oxford scientist Richard Dawkins (but see below, pp. 37–39) certainly takes the view that our genes are the overriding determinant of what we are (Dawkins 1995: 155): 'The universe we observe has precisely the properties we should expect if there is, at bottom, no design, no purpose, no evil, no good, nothing but blind pitiless indifference ... DNA neither cares nor knows. DNA just is. And we dance to its music.' But is this true?

The biological nature of humankind

The Bible is very clear that human life originates in God. The apostle Paul summarized it neatly when he addressed the philosophers and academics of Athens: 'For in him we live and move and have our being' (Acts 17:28). God is the creator and sustainer of *all* life.

This is what the opening chapters of the Bible, Genesis 1 and 2, are discussing. They are not setting out the biological methods involved in the creation of human beings; for that we look to current scientific evidence, which points very strongly indeed towards an evolutionary process. In holding this view we align ourselves with the majority of Christian biologists and biomedical scientists, who, having very carefully evaluated the data in the light of their faith, reach the conclusion that the evidence for the process of evolution is

3. The song 'My Sweet Lord' was, sadly, not about Jesus Christ but about Krishna.

overwhelming. This conclusion does not diminish our view of God; rather, as for other Christian biologists (one of many examples is Wright, 1989), it increases our awe at the magnificence of the creative process.

Humankind, *Homo sapiens*, is no exception to what we have just said. Biologically, humans are mammals: warm-blooded animals with fur that nurture their embryos within the body of the female and that suckle their young. The mammalian nature of humans is shown by the number of genes we share with rodents – genes that specify the essential features of mammals. Our nearest living relatives are the great apes, especially the chimpanzees. However, on our evolutionary pathway the chimpanzee route and the human route diverged at least 5 million years ago. A Christian cell biologist, Finlay (2003), has recently documented many of the genetic differences between us and other primates, showing some of the specific genetic changes that have occurred at each divergence along the evolutionary pathway: from the general primate route to the great-ape route to the *Homo* route. 'Modern' human beings, members of the species *Homo sapiens*, are currently thought to have originated from a very small population of immediately 'pre-human' ancestors that survived in Africa during the period in which what is now Europe was experiencing a major ice age (see Oppenheimer, 2003). Indeed, that population was so small that some anthropologists believe that all humans can trace their genetic lineage back to a single female who lived in Africa, probably about 150,000 years ago. This putative female ancestor has been called the 'mitochondrial Eve' because of the particular genes used to trace the lineage.

The exact time in prehistory at which we can identify modern humans is a matter for conjecture. If the small population in Africa was indeed human, the dating would be 150,000 years ago. Some scholars, however, basing their thesis on particular forms of art, suggest that humans, as we understand the term, may have appeared as recently as 50,000 years ago. Scholars who opt for the earlier dating suggest that it was between 50,000 and 40,000 years ago that 'Europe' was first colonized (Oppenheimer, 2003). In any case, in evolutionary terms all these time scales are short, a mere fraction of the time since the divergence from the great-ape evolutionary pathway.

In respect of our common ancestry with the great apes, albeit a very long time ago, much has often been made of the very close similarity between the genetic make-up of humans and that of chimpanzees. In terms of DNA we differ from our distant 'cousins' by less than 2%. Further, some of the gene changes that led to that apparently small difference have been documented (see Finlay, 2003). Finlay is, however, at pains to emphasize that the genetic changes that have led to *Homo sapiens* define not what it is to be human but only the specific biological nature of humans; the genetic changes are only part of the story. As the evolutionary psychologist Steven Pinker has pointed out (Pinker, 2000), the genetic differences between humans and chimpanzees may be small but the differences between their 'lifestyles' are enormous. Chimpanzees are in reality a threatened species living in a restricted habitat in the tropics. The human species has grown to a population of 6,400 million and has tamed (or found ways of living in) most of the world's habitats. The same dominance also means that the human species has the power to despoil or destroy. Many of its society groups are complex and, as individuals or as groups, humans participate in complex activities that are not directly related to biological survival.

We may point to two specific features of humans that led to all this. The first is the size of the brain and the second is the development of speech and then language. Both Pinker (2000) and the philosopher Chomsky (for a recent example see Chomsky, 2000) rate language as the major defining feature of human behaviour because it led to so much more. Pinker actually goes farther than this, to suggest that language is such a key feature in our natural selection that human infants' brains are hard-wired specifically to learn language in the early years of life. Oppenheimer (2003) also agrees that speech, leading to the development of real language, is a uniquely human feature.

This is not the place to discuss the relationships between brain, mind, consciousness and thought. Nevertheless, it is clear that the development of the human brain makes possible complex processes of mind that we do not see in even our closest relatives. We have a high level of consciousness – of self-awareness – and we are, in the main, capable of abstract thought and of conveying abstract ideas in language. We have what Robert Winston (Winston, 2003) calls 'imagination': the ability to perceive and think about things that are not part of our immediate physical surroundings, or indeed within our experience. He and others cite the occurrence of burial rituals as evidence of thought about the possibility of a life beyond this one. That quality of imagination is also apparent in artistic representations of animals and hunting scenes that could not have been present at the site at which the artist was working (after all, many of these early paintings were done in caves). Further, in humans we see a moral dimension: an ability to choose between right and wrong that is much more than the biological altruism exhibited by certain animals. Now, we do not wish to indulge in speculation about how and when early humans came to bear God's image – to be spiritual beings – but it is clear that some of the uniquely human qualities we have mentioned here are entirely compatible with that image.

How do these human qualities relate to our genetic make-up? The development of a human person from a single cell is an awesome process. It involves an interplay of some 30,000 genes, each with specific and often subtle regulatory mechanisms and responses to external and internal cues and signals. Overall this interplay has a complexity that we can scarcely imagine. This wonderful set of processes starts with the fertilized egg and leads, via the establishment of a proper embryo, to the production of an independently functioning human person with about 70 million million cells. It is obvious that as far as genes go, all the genetic information needed for this developmental process and for 'running' a human being must exist in the fertilized egg.

For some writers, that is it: genes are everything. In the UK, Dawkins has been in the past, as already mentioned, an articulate proponent of genetic reductionism or determinism, the theory that all the qualities that we have ascribed to humans are the outworkings of their genes. Others, such as the science journalist Matt Ridley (e.g. 1994, 1997), have also enthusiastically espoused this view. In the USA its most vociferous supporters are Dennett (e.g. 1995), E. O. Wilson (e.g. 1978, 1998) and Pinker (despite the latter's insistence that the apparently small genetic differences between chimpanzees and humans tell only part of the story). On this view, everything humans are and do – their aesthetic sense, their moral make-up, their emotional life, their spirituality[4] and so on – is determined by their genes. That is not to say that these writers take a simplistic view of the relationship between genes and behaviour. They would not, for

---

4. Dawkins combines his genetic reductionist philosophy with a hatred of religion (see, for example, the recent anthology of his work, *A Devil's Chaplain*: Dawkins, 2003), which leads him to be a particularly strident critic and opponent of Christianity.

example, talk about a 'gay gene'. Nevertheless, for them genes are *the* biological authority.

Space does not permit a detailed critique of this genetic reductionism. Readers who wish for a fuller treatment are referred to Holmes Rolston's withering, and in places very witty, analysis of E. O. Wilson's view of altruism (Rolston, 1999, especially pp. 252–256) and to Roger Forster's and Paul Marston's discussion of the work of Dawkins and Dennett (Forster and Marston, 1999). Here we confine ourselves to two points. First, even at the biological level genes do not govern everything that happens, as is often pointed out by the atheist biologist Steven Rose (e.g. Rose, 1997). For example, the establishment of neuronal connections, whether in development or in the learning experiences of everyday life, cannot be genetically determined. Secondly, some of the proponents of genetic reductionism find it impossible to live with their views. Thus Dawkins has proposed, and reiterated over a quarter of a century (see Dawkins, 2003, especially pp. 117–151), that social and cultural values are inherited by entities called 'memes' that are capable of passing from one brain to another and that religion is a kind of social virus that infects the memes. This is an interesting view, but in evaluating it we need to ask what specific evidence there is to support it, especially in the light of his many antagonistic comments on religion. For instance:

> To describe religions as mind viruses is sometimes interpreted as contemptuous or even hostile. It is both. I am often asked why I am so hostile to 'organized religion'. My first response is that I am not exactly friendly towards disorganized religion either. As a lover of truth, *I am suspicious of strongly held beliefs that are unsupported by evidence* (Dawkins, 2003: 117; italics added).

The strong espousal of the idea of memes and meme-viruses is interesting in the light of the italicized words in this quotation.

Dawkins (e.g. 1993, 1999, 2003) also proposes that, although we are genetically determined, it is our privilege as humans to overcome the deterministic activity of our genes. Our readers will certainly readily identify the weakness in the argument. Similarly, Dennett (2003) has recently written that human free will has evolved as part of our natural selection, while Matt Ridley (2003a) now concedes that influences other than genes play a large part in our emotional and social development. In commenting on these more recent publications Steven Rose (2003) refers to the authors as penitents who are now seeing the error of their ways!

A more balanced scientific view, therefore, is that the profile of our adult lives is determined by a mixture of nature and nurture: our genetic disposition, our environment, our upbringing and our experience (see also Chapters 6 and 7). Helpful as this is in confronting us with the responsibility of shaping our own lives, it neither unpacks what is meant by such phrases as 'the sanctity of life' nor answers George Harrison's questions. We thus ask: is there more?

What are human beings? The biblical perspective[5]

It is of course to the Bible that Christians turn as they seek to answer the question 'What are human beings?' Indeed, this is a question that frequently preoccupies Scripture. As he surveys the vastness of the heaven above him the psalmist (Ps. 8:4) asks:

What is man that you are mindful of him,
the son of man that you care for him?

The influence of Christian thought is wider than one might imagine. Our legislation has been guided by the Judaeo-Christian tradition for centuries, even though society has often been slow to see its full implications and so has happily tolerated slavery for 1,800 years, or supported racial segregation or the poor treatment of the disabled. These failures to understand and apply biblical principles do not in any way invalidate those principles, and it is to the Bible that Christians turn in seeking to answer the fundamental questions about the nature of humankind.

The foundation texts are in Genesis 1:26–27 and 2:7.[6] The first passage reads:

Then God said, 'Let us make humankind in our image, according to our likeness; and let them have dominion over the

---

5. There is a huge literature on this subject. One of the clearest and most inspiring recent expositions is John Wyatt's book *Matters of Life and Death* (Wyatt, 1998).

6. Here we use the NRSV.

fish of the sea, and over the birds of the air, and over the cattle, and over all the wild animals of the earth, and over every creeping thing that creeps upon the earth.'

> So God created humankind in his image,
>   in the image of God he created them;
>   male and female he created them.

Genesis 2:7 adds: 'the LORD God formed man from the dust of the ground and breathed into his nostrils the breath of life; and the man became a living being.' What do these texts tell us about the biblical view of human beings? What are we?

First, we are made by God. God said, 'Let us make', and so God created human beings; and in the Genesis 2 account he 'formed man from the dust of the ground'. These three verbs – made, created, formed – all speak of God crafting human beings. In other words, human beings did not emerge by chance; they are the outcome of God's intention and activity. (Our evolutionary perspective is entirely compatible with these statements and does not in any way diminish the vital importance of these chapters in understanding the nature of human beings.) God is, then, the source of human life. With him is the 'fountain of life' (Ps. 36:9). In him 'we live and move and have our being' (Acts 17:28).

Secondly, human beings are the crown of God's creation. In Genesis 1 humans are made as the completion of the created order. In Genesis 2, the man is shown as the peak of God's creation by the responsibility given to him by God of naming the animals and birds. Adam is the divinely appointed taxonomist! We are part of the biological creation; as molecular biology has shown, DNA is the intrinsic component of all living organisms. But God has also set humans apart from creation by giving them a spiritual nature not conferred on other creatures. He 'breathed into his nostrils the breath of life; and the man became a living being'. We are more than our biology.

Thirdly, we are made in the image and likeness of God. This does not mean we are identical to God; we are a reflection, a created analogy, to whom he may reveal himself, with whom he can enter into relationship, and in whom he may be glorified. This is not to suggest that the image of God lies primarily in our reason, creativity, speech or spiritual nature, but rather that the whole person – body, mind and spirit – bears the image of God. Humankind is the corporeal image of the incorporeal God, but only in Christ is that image perfectly revealed: 'He is the image of the invisible God, the firstborn over all creation' (Col. 1:15).

Fourthly, we are made male and female. God declares his intention to make human beings in his own image, but there follow not one creature but two: 'So God created humankind in his image, in the image of God he created them; male and female he created them' (Gen. 1:27). The expression of the divine image in human beings requires both sexes, male and female. While each individual person bears the image of God, the full expression of that image is seen in the relationships between men and women. This implies a fundamental equality between men and women.

Fifthly, being made in God's image implies being made for relationships. At first glance, Genesis 1:26 is curious: 'Let us make humankind in our image, according to our likeness.' Here there may be the seeds of the Trinitarian nature of God, which unfolds in Scripture. God is three persons in one God, equal in relationship with one another but assigning different functions among them. The intimacy of this relationship is seen, for example, in the later chapters of John's Gospel. Jesus explains to his disciples that he is going to return to his Father, with whom he is one. But he will send them the Spirit from the Father, and he will be their divine helper (John 16:4–11). Indeed, the only way to know what God the Father is like is to look at Jesus, the Son (John 14:9). It is the Spirit that guides them into the truth of this and into all truth (John 16:13). To be made in the image of God is therefore to be made to be in relationships of equality with others but fulfilling the roles and responsibilities assigned to us individually.

Lastly, then, to be made in the image of God is to be given responsibilities. The first of these is to procreate: 'God blessed them, and God said to them, "Be fruitful and multiply"' (Gen. 1:28, NRSV). This is the mechanism by which God's image is to be passed on from one generation to another. Chapter 5 of Genesis lists the descendants of the representative man, Adam, who was made 'in the likeness of God'. His son, Seth, is made in the likeness of his father, Adam (Gen. 5:1–3), and so the procedure goes on down the line. The second responsibility assigned to human beings by God is stewardship of the earth, not for personal gain but for the provision of human need. God has provided every plant for food (Gen. 1:28–30).

Similarly, the work God gives Adam to do in the Garden of Eden is to 'till [the ground] and keep it' (2:15, NRSV).

The biblical answer to the psalmist's question, 'What are human beings?', to George Harrison's search and to the age-old cry, 'Who am I?' is that each and every human person originates in God and is made in God's likeness, to be in relationship with other human beings and to discharge the responsibilities God has given us. Herein is the essence of the sacredness of human life: that each individual is crafted by God, infinitely precious, not because of our achievements but because God made us to be like him.

But there are obvious problems in understanding what it means to be human in this way. If being human depends on our ability to form relationships, to give and receive love, to think and make decisions, to work and to do; if these are the defining marks of what it means to be made in the image of God; if these are the attributes which confer sacredness on human life, we are in danger of relegating to a lower order those who are unable to engage in such things. Many people are, to varying degrees, prevented from exhibiting these characteristics by disease or accident which causes serious impairment of neurological and/or psychological function. The biblical order is here of crucial importance. What makes human life special, and separates us from the rest of the creation, is not what *we* do but what *God* has done, namely that he made, created, formed us to be in his likeness. Therein lies the essential dignity of every man and woman.

Furthermore, God has a particular concern for the weak and vulnerable which he expects us also to exercise. This is a thread that runs throughout Scripture, which we highlight with but a few examples. God takes the trouble and grief of the helpless and orphans into his own hands (Ps. 10:14). He has pity on the weak and the needy (Ps. 72:13). The prophets complain that God's people flagrantly disobey him in this matter and will therefore be subject to his severe judgment (Amos 2:6). God saves the lame and the outcast (Zeph. 3:19). Jesus' own ministry was not only one of teaching but also one of showing compassion to the sick and disabled. He made clear that in meeting the needs of the sick and disadvantaged we are in fact doing that to him; conversely, to ignore them is to ignore him (Matt. 25:31–46). The evidence of true religion is to be seen not only in moral purity but also in caring for those upon whom society places little value (Jas. 1:27). Any suggestion that the disabled and weak are something less than human is utterly refuted by the

Scriptures. It is actually their vulnerability that places them under God's special care, which is to be reflected in our attitude towards them. Thus any suggestion that people who are disabled in any way are less than fully human or in some way a lesser expression of God's image is utterly incompatible with the teaching of the Bible and cannot therefore be entertained by Christians. This Christian understanding of what we are has been succinctly expressed by Archbishop William Temple (1941: 74): 'My worth is what I am worth to God; and that is a marvellous great deal, for Christ died for me.'

The fall has distorted God's image in human beings because of human disobedience to God. Sin has defiled what God had made good so that we are a mixture of glory and tragedy. John Stott has expressed this with his customary clarity in his book *The Cross of Christ* (1986). In the chapter in which he addresses our human self-understanding he writes (p. 284):

> There is, therefore, a great need for discernment in our self-understanding, Who am I? What is my 'self'? The answer is I am a Jekyll and Hyde, a mixed-up kid, having both dignity, because I was created and have been re-created in the image of God, and depravity, because I still have a fallen and rebellious nature. I am both noble and ignoble, beautiful and ugly, good and bad, upright and twisted, image and child of God, and yet sometimes yielding obsequious homage to the devil.

On the one hand, therefore, human beings are entitled to respect, dignity and protection, because we are all made in the image of God; but on the other hand we need to be saved, because sin has defaced that image. As we have already seen in Chapter 2, the salvation process includes the transforming work of the Holy Spirit to make like Christ those who follow Christ. This is magnificently summarized by the apostle Paul in his second letter to the Christians at Corinth: 'And all of us with unveiled faces, seeing the glory of the Lord as though reflected in a mirror, are being transformed into the same image from one degree of glory to another; for this comes from the Lord, the Spirit' (2 Cor. 3:18, NRSV).

Finally, Scripture is clear that human life continues beyond our present experience of it. It is given by God and will return to God. The last chapter of Ecclesiastes graphically describes the increasing frailty of old age and concludes with the bald statement that 'the dust

returns to the earth as it was and the spirit returns to God who gave it'
(12:7). The long-term objective of the saving work of Christ through
his incarnation, cross and resurrection is that we shall indeed return
to God, who is the originator and creator of human life, that 'we will
be with the Lord for ever' (1 Thess. 4:17).

In summary, human beings are made in the image of God and all
that that implies. But they are also in need of redemption and
transformation. All of this originates in God, is given by God and is
carried through by God. The sacred essence of being human is that
humans are objects of divine grace. It is upon this basis that the Bible
obliges us to nurture and care for human life and places constraints
on what we may do with it. Thus nobody may use another human
being for his or her own ends without consent.

This is well expressed in Immanuel Kant's 'categorical imperatives'. Kant combined his religious views with the idea that general
moral precepts (or categorical imperatives) could be derived by
human reason. One of his imperatives was that no human should
be used instrumentally by another. Christians of course recognize
and, it is hoped, follow this precept in the form of the second great
commandment of Jesus, that we should love our neighbours as
ourselves. Vengeful killing is forbidden and murder is outlawed. But
do these constraints include an absolute prohibition on taking
human life? In Old Testament times there were clear exceptions to
the commandment 'You shall not kill': the death penalty was applied
for certain offences and enemies were often exterminated. Jesus,
however, presented us with a completely different approach: he
commanded us to love our enemies and to bless those who persecute
us. Even so, there are many Christians who believe that taking a
human life may in some circumstances be a more virtuous action
than not doing so: for example, to prevent grievous harm being done
to others. Many Christians who fought against Germany in the
Second World War believed that war was the only option,[7] and
the German pastor Dietrich Bonhoeffer participated in a plot to kill
Hitler. On the other hand, there are Christians who hold that the
killing of other humans, including that which occurs in just wars, is
always wrong. The latter topic is discussed in depth by Hays (1996).

---

7. With hindsight, we note that many aspects of the Second World War fell far
short of the standards implicit in just-war theory, especially in the targeting of
non-combatants.

He reaches the conclusion that there is no justification for killing others and believes that the commands of Jesus should lead us to pacifism, nevertheless acknowledging that many Christians will thoughtfully and prayerfully reach other conclusions.

These debates about human life have been brought into even sharper focus over the last twenty-five years by developments in molecular biology and medicine. We can manipulate genes. We can fertilize human eggs in the laboratory, thereby creating embryos for therapeutic and research purposes. But are embryos thus created human beings subject to the same care and constraints which Scripture confers on the postnatal human? It is to this vexed question we must now turn.

Can we actually know what is the relationship between the person developing in the womb and the image of God? If, from fertilization onwards, the developing person is indeed in the image of God, Christians must say that the only possible investigation, intervention or treatment to which it may be subjected, at any time, must be for its own benefit. This has been at the heart of the debate surrounding medical advances over the last fifty years, beginning with the 1967 Abortion Act, via the birth of Louise Brown (the first 'test-tube baby') in 1978, to more recent advances in artificial reproduction and research on the early human embryo.

The status of the human embryo

Termination of pregnancy
How do we view the unborn child? Before 1967, abortion, the termination of pregnancy, was unlawful except in cases where it was performed in good faith to save the life of the mother. 'Back-street' abortions were common, as were a variety of methods used by women to induce a miscarriage. These were at times fatal and they also posed a serious threat to the future health of women, particularly through infection and rendering it more difficult to conceive subsequently. David Steele's 1967 Abortion Act was a humane attempt to protect the health of women. Under the Act, abortion is lawful if two doctors, acting in good faith, agree that the pregnancy would involve one or more of the following:

- A risk to the life of the mother

- A risk of injury to her or her children's physical or mental health greater than if the pregnancy were terminated
- A substantial risk that if the child were born it would suffer from physical or mental abnormalities so as to be seriously handicapped

In 1990, the upper time limit for abortion was reduced from twenty-eight weeks to twenty-four weeks, but there is *no* limit if there is a substantial risk that the child will be born with a serious mental or physical handicap. Although the Act lays down the circumstances under which abortion is lawful, it has been interpreted by doctors and public alike so that in practice the indication for abortion is that the mother does not wish the pregnancy to continue. In the first twenty years of the Act's operation in England and Wales some 3 million abortions were carried out. It is estimated that in the USA there are 1.5 million abortions each year. This is abortion on demand. It reflects the prevailing ethical basis of decision-making in the Western world in the twenty-first century: namely, the ethics of rights (see Chapter 2). It is considered to be a woman's right to decide whether or not she wishes to have the child with which she is pregnant.

Together with Christians of most other traditions, we believe such an approach to be wrong. However much it may be sanitized, abortion on demand is the killing, because it is not wanted, of an unborn child who is recognizably human and, if allowed to come to birth, would most probably grow into a healthy adult. Mother Teresa called it murder. There is, however, a divergence of view about the morality of terminating pregnancy if its continuation poses a risk to the life of the mother. The official Roman Catholic view is that the life of the unborn child should take precedence over the life of the mother, while Protestants tend to favour the life of the mother. Exodus 21:22 is often brought into this argument: 'When people who are fighting injure a pregnant woman so that there is a miscarriage, and yet no further harm follows, the one responsible shall be fined what the woman's husband demands, paying as much as the judges determine' (NRSV). In our view this is not helpful, because the passage is notoriously unclear. It is not clear whether it refers specifically to a miscarriage or to the early delivery of a child, induced incidentally following a violent quarrel. It does not set out to assess the relative values of the lives of a mother and her unborn child. The question of terminating a pregnancy if the child is going to be seriously physically or mentally handicapped is more difficult. We discuss this in more detail in Chapter 6.

In vitro *fertilization and the status of the embryo*

These arguments were well rehearsed before the 1967 Act was passed and the debate, often fierce and strident, continues. However, an entirely new dimension was introduced in 1978 following the birth of Louise Brown, the world's first 'test-tube' baby. Louise was born following the work of two British researchers, Steptoe, a gynaecologist, and Edwards, a Cambridge scientist. They succeeded in fertilizing a woman's egg with a man's sperm, in the laboratory. Several embryos were thus created and one was successfully implanted into Louise's mother's uterus. The creation of 'spare' embryos (that is, embryos which would not be implanted and would in effect be wasted) was, and remains, an essential part of the technique. This technique has formed the basis of several further developments over the last twenty-five years: embryo research, pre-implantation diagnosis, embryo selection, and embryo creation for the production of stem cells, all of which are discussed in Chapters 6 and 8.

Many people, both Christian and non-Christian, were profoundly disturbed by this technology, raising such questions as, 'What is the status of the early embryo prior to its implantation into the lining of the womb?' 'Is it a human being or just a group of cells?' 'Is it a potential human life?' 'What protection should be given to it?' 'Is it yet imbued with the image of God?' A quarter of a century later, Christians and others are seriously divided over the answers to these questions and therefore about what is right and wrong in this area. Within the church, some would like to make it a test of orthodox belief. We approach the subject with some trepidation and a sense of inadequacy. Our own conclusions, to which we come later in this chapter, will be unacceptable to some, whereas others will have no difficulty in agreeing with them. On the one hand, there are debates about what the Bible teaches and the church's understanding of it. On the other hand, there is the reality of finding effective treatments for some diseases and preventing suffering in others. We shall attempt to find a way through these difficult matters by:

- Summarizing the present law in England and Wales
- Reviewing the approach of Christians over the centuries

- Examining the views that human life begins at fertilization or at implantation
- Drawing our conclusions

The law in England and Wales

In response to the concerns following the birth of Louise Brown, the Government set up a committee, chaired by the distinguished philosopher Mary Warnock, to examine the issues and make recommendations. The Warnock Committee reported in 1984. It took the view that the key stage in prenatal human development was not fertilization but implantation, although there was a dissenting minority report. The Report formed the basis of the legislation that set up the Human Fertilization and Embryology Authority (HFEA) in 1990. The Authority regulates work and developments in this area of science and medicine. The Act has five main provisions:

- The HFEA supervises all activity related to human reproductive technology. All these activities must take place under licence granted by the Authority.
- Embryo donation and donor insemination are acceptable, subject to licence. The Act also sets out who are the lawful parents of children conceived by artificial reproduction and the confidentiality arrangements about genetic parents.
- Embryos and sperms can be frozen. They may be used at a future date with the consent of the donors. They are destroyed after ten years.
- The Act sets out the legislative framework within which surrogacy arrangements may be made.
- Research on human embryos up to fourteen days after fertilization is allowed under licence. The specific purposes for which research may be performed are:
  - Promoting advances in understanding infertility
  - Gaining knowledge about congenital disease
  - The development of contraceptive techniques
  - Detecting gene and chromosome abnormalities

More recent legislation has added to this list permission for the production of embryos for the purposes of stem-cell research (Chapter 8) and, on a case-by-case basis, the selection of a sibling for the treatment of a child already born (Chapter 6).

The activities carried out under licence from the HFEA continue to be regarded by some Christians and other groups as unethical. However, the majority view among those who enshrine public policy in legislation is that these activities both confer benefit and prevent suffering. The legislation is therefore unlikely to be rescinded. Sometimes those who disapprove of work in these areas regard those who undertake it as being devoid of ethical principles and having scant regard for human life. This is far from the truth. The vast majority of workers in this field have a very high regard for the sacredness of human life and it is actually this that motivates them to relieve suffering and promote health through these technologies.

Historical approach

The status and protection afforded to the unborn child has been a matter of debate for more than two thousand years. The main points of the debate are well known and will be only summarized here. Aristotle developed the idea of the unborn child as formed or unformed. It was 'formed' when it was recognizably human, which was said to be forty days after conception in the case of a male and ninety days for a female. It was at these points that human status could be conferred on the child, because this was considered to be the point of 'ensoulment'.

Many of the early Church Fathers took the view that abortion was wrong, but gave different reasons. Basil of Caesarea held that it was irrelevant whether the child was formed or unformed. His brother, Gregory of Nyssa, thought differently. He did not regard the unformed unborn child as having human status, although he still held that the destruction of unborn life at any stage was morally unacceptable, even if it did not always amount to murder. This view prevailed until the sixteenth century, when Pope Sixtus V decreed that abortion was murder at whatever stage it was performed. Within ten years, however, his successor but one, Gregory XIV, reinstated Gregory of Nyssa's view. The absolutist view of Sixtus V was reaffirmed in the papal Bull of 1869 and has remained the official Roman Catholic view. The Encyclical Letter *Evangelium Vitae* of John Paul II, issued in 1995, states (104) that 'procured abortion is the deliberate and direct killing, by whatever means it is carried out, of a human being in the initial phase of his or her existence, extending from conception to birth'.

The debate within the wider church

Outside the Roman Catholic Church there is also a huge literature on this subject. Within the evangelical constituency, Berry (1993), Jones (1984), McCarthy (1997), Moore (2001), O'Donovan (1984), P. Taylor (2002) and Wyatt (1998), among others, have all written about it with clarity and scholarship, seeking to find the biblical view. Their books are worth reading in detail. We note that among these authors there are differing views on the status of the early human embryo. Here we summarize the two main positions in the debate, namely (a) that human life begins at fertilization or (b) that human life begins at implantation. As a prelude to this discussion we note that the term 'human life' is being used here as shorthand: those who believe that implantation is the major event that informs our view of the status of the early embryo would not deny that the pre-implantation embryo is in some sense 'human life'. It is the significance ascribed to that life that is actually under debate.

Human life begins at fertilization

Advocates of the view that human life begins at fertilization point to a number of biblical texts which apply personal language to the human embryo or suggest a personal relationship with God before birth (Job 3:3; Pss. 22:9–10; 51:5; 58:3; 139:13–16), which suggest that God may call individuals before birth (Is. 49:1, 5; Jer. 1:5; Gal. 1:15), and in which God distinguishes between people before birth (Gen. 25:22–24; Rom. 9:10–13) (McCarthy, 1997: 60–88). Nevertheless, Psalm 139:1–18 (here from NRSV) is probably for many the most familiar biblical statement about prenatal life:

> O LORD, you have searched me and known me.
> You know when I sit down and when I rise up;
>   you discern my thoughts from far away.
> You search out my path and my lying down,
>   and are acquainted with all my ways.
> Even before a word is on my tongue,
>   O LORD, you know it completely.
> You hem me in, behind and before,
>   and lay your hand upon me.
> Such knowledge is too wonderful for me;
>   it is so high that I cannot attain it.

Where can I go from your spirit?
  Or where can I flee from your presence?
If I ascend to heaven, you are there;
  if I make my bed in Sheol, you are there.
If I take the wings of the morning
  and settle at the farthest limits of the sea,
even there your hand shall lead me,
  and your right hand shall hold me fast.
If I say, 'Surely the darkness shall cover me,
  and the light around me become night,'
even the darkness is not dark to you;
  the night is as bright as the day,
  for darkness is as light to you.

For it was you who formed my inward parts;
  you knit me together in my mother's womb.
I praise you, for I am fearfully and wonderfully made.
  Wonderful are your works;
that I know very well.
  My frame was not hidden from you,
when I was being made in secret,
  intricately woven in the depths of the earth.
Your eyes beheld my unformed substance.
In your book were written
  all the days that were formed for me,
  when none of them as yet existed.
How weighty to me are your thoughts, O God!
  How vast is the sum of them!
I try to count them – they are more than the sand;
  I come to the end – I am still with you.

The main points we can take from this are:

- *Creation*. We are created by God: 'you [God] who formed my
  inward parts [and] knit me together in my mother's womb' (13).
  God formed, shaped, modelled the psalmist in his mother's
  womb. The process of prenatal development is God's creative
  work (Stott, 1999). It is for this, his creation in the womb, that
  the psalmist thanks God (14): 'I praise you, for I am fearfully and

wonderfully made.' Similar ideas are found throughout Scripture: e.g. Job 10:8–11.

- *Continuity.* Our human life is a continuous personal thread. The psalmist reflects on God's continuous work, knitting him together in his mother's womb (13), searching out and knowing him before and since he was born (1), his present knowledge of him (2–3) and his future guidance. God's activity on his behalf extends from his prenatal existence and then on throughout his life.
- *Covenant.* The psalmist also speaks of God's constant presence with him. No matter where he is, God leads and holds him. God is committed to him from the days of his 'unformed substance' right through to the 'days that were formed for me' (see Stott, 1999: 354–359).

It is this understanding of the creative work of God, his continuous concern and his commitment of grace to individuals, which can be traced back to the beginning of their existence, that persuades some that human life begins at fertilization. This view is not compatible with any concept of personhood being gradual; rather, personhood is conferred at the precise moment at which in our early embryonic life we become made in the image of God. Proponents of this view may also be uneasy about the language of 'potential': that the fertilized egg has the potential for personhood. Personhood is said to be present at the moment of fusion of the sperm and the egg (actually not a precisely defined moment but a process over several hours). Even though the attributes of personhood will become apparent only later, through prenatal and postnatal development, we must commit ourselves to the care and protection of the embryo from its very earliest stage, because God is so committed. Taken to its logical conclusion this view makes it very difficult for an infertile couple to have a child using currently available techniques of artificial reproduction.[8] Furthermore, any intervention in an embryo is ethical only if the intervention is for the benefit of that embryo alone. No other form of intervention can be allowed (see discussion on donor embryos in Chapter 6).

---

8. Unless no spare embryos are created during each attempt at *in vitro* fertilization and each embryo thus created is inserted into the uterus with a view to establishing a pregnancy.

Those who hold this view might also argue that it is supported by science: for example, that all the genetic information for the development of a person is present from fertilization, and after this, it is suggested, there is no clear point of interruption in the life of the embryo or foetus.

Human life begins at implantation

We again need to remind our readers that we are using shorthand: of course the pre-implantation embryo is biologically human. The question is about whether we should ascribe human personhood to it, with all that would imply. The view that human life begins at implantation seeks to understand Scripture in the light of the modern understanding of science. We must therefore begin this particular part of the discussion with seeing what happens in the early stages of embryonic development.

The egg and the sperm each contain one copy of their generators' genes. When the sperm and the egg meet, fertilization takes place, involving the gradual fusion of the two cells over a period of several hours. The fertilized egg ('zygote' or one-celled embryo) then possesses the full double complement of human DNA and contains all the genetic information that will be needed for the development and life of a human being.[9] For several days, the early embryo moves down the fallopian tubes and then into the womb itself. Cell division occurs during this time, during which the cells of the embryo are developmentally uncommitted. At this early stage we cannot even determine which cells will go on, after further divisions, to form the embryo proper and which will form the placenta. Indeed, it is possible, as discussed in Chapter 6, to remove a cell at the eight-cell stage for genetic testing. The seven remaining cells will develop normally.

Eventually a hollow ball of cells called the blastocyst is formed. Inside the blastocyst, attached to its outer wall of cells, is an inner group of cells sometimes called the blastocoel (see Figure 3.1). It is only at this stage of development that we can discern any future developmental direction: if a pregnancy is established, the outer cell layers will become the placenta and the inner cell mass the embryo itself. However, it is by no means certain that the blastocyst will

---

9. It is important to note that, while this genetic information is totally *necessary*, it is not *sufficient* for the development and life of a human.

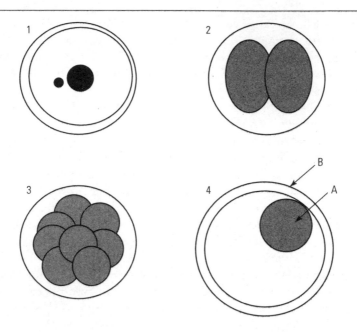

1. Shortly after the penetration of the egg by a single sperm cell, the two nuclei, each containing one set of genes, are clearly visible. Note that although the two nuclei contain equivalent amounts of DNA, the egg cell nucleus is much bigger than the sperm cell nucleus. The complete fusion of the two nuclei and the activation of the fertilized egg to divide will take about ten more hours.

2. The first cell division has taken place (note that the nuclei are not shown in diagrams 2–4).

3. After two more rounds of cell division the embryo is at the uncompacted eight-cell stage.

4. The blastocyst stage. The embryo now consists of an inner mass of cells (A) and an outer layer of cells (B).

Figure 3.1. Early development of the human embryo

develop further. Many early embryos simply do not survive. Of those that do go on to implant into the wall of the womb and thus establish a pregnancy (see below), a proportion will divide into two at around the time of implantation and thus become identical twins. There is also evidence that, rarely, two separate embryos may merge; if those two embryos have arisen from fertilization of two eggs, the resulting human will be a genetic mosaic.

At around the stage of thirty to sixty cells, up to ten days after fertilization, the blastocyst begins to attach itself to the wall of the womb. As this happens certain hormonal changes occur in the mother and she misses her monthly period and begins to 'feel pregnant'. The placenta is formed by growth of the outer layer of blastocyst cells, and the totipotent[10] cells of the blastocoel begin to form the embryo proper. At around fourteen days the cells become more organized and the primitive streak, a strip of cells which is the precursor of the central nervous system, appears; by ten or eleven weeks organs have been formed and early limbs are also present.

It is the point of implantation that many people regard as the key stage in the development of the human embryo, for several reasons:

- Although all the genetic information for the development of a human being is present from fertilization, it is not until implantation that the developmental potential may be realized. The embryo needs to form a physical relationship, essentially a parasitic relationship, with the mother in order for its development, including the 'interpretation' of its genetic information, to be supported. We do need to add, however, that it is not clear whether it is implantation itself that induces further development. The very rare occurrence of ectopic pregnancy (implantation of the embryo in the wrong place, generally the fallopian tube) shows that attachment to the mother can take place outside the uterus. The even rarer instances of an ectopic pregnancy coming to term (ectopic pregnancies would generally be fatal for the mother, so usually they are terminated) show that development can be sustained in the 'wrong' place. The key is the physical linkage to the mother via the placenta: without it, the genetic complement of the embryo would be useless; development would not take place. There is, however, active research aimed at achieving ectogenesis: full development of the embryo/foetus outside of the womb. This would certainly bring its own ethical challenges but would not alter the view of those who regard implantation as a very significant milestone (any more than IVF alters the view of those who regard fertilization as the significant milestone).
- The formation of the placenta is a vital part of embryonic development and, as we have briefly mentioned already, it is only

---

10. Capable of giving rise to all the different types of cell in the body.

at the blastocyst stage that we distinguish future embryo/foetus[11] from future placenta. Obviously the placenta is necessary for the survival and growth of the unborn child, but it is difficult to regard it as human except in the sense of being human biological material. So what is the status of those early cells which develop into it?

- About 70% of fertilized eggs do not implant: they are lost via the vagina. What is the status of these early embryos? Are they human life until they perish? They certainly contain a unique complement of DNA but this is irrelevant if further development does not occur. What then is our Christian reponsibility towards them?

The conclusion of those who believe, as we do, that life begins at implantation is that Psalm 139 speaks not of all embryos but of known humans who are the objects of God's creative love, continuous care and covenant grace. It is written from the vantage point of life which looks back and sees the gracious hand of God upon us from before we were born. Just as Genesis 1 and 2 should not be used to tell us how the universe was created, so Psalm 139 should not be used to tell us about early embryonic development (see also the concluding discussion at the end of this chapter).

As is so often the case in disagreements among Christians about what Scripture teaches, there is a difference in hermeneutics. In this case it is difficult to see how these differences can be reconciled. To the one group, the pre-implantation embryo is a human person, called by God and made in his image, whose very vulnerability should elicit our protection. True, it does not yet have many of the attributes of a human being, but the tension between the 'now' and the 'not yet' is a familiar biblical theme and its application to the early human embryo should not surprise us. To the other group, the pluripotential nature of the early embryo's cells, its extreme precariousness before implantation and the fact that one embryo can become two persons or that two embryos can become one person make it unlikely that Scripture requires us to regard the early embryo as a human person. Rather, it has the potential to become a living

---

11. Although biologists tend to use the term *embryo* at all stages of pregnancy, it is usual medical parlance, when referring to human pregnancy, to use the term *foetus* to denote embryos older than about eight weeks.

human being, provided that a relationship with the mother is established via implantation.

Concluding discussion

As we have shown in this discussion, there are two main views of the status of the early human embryo and its relationship to human personhood and to the image of God. Those who hold these different views do so with equal sincerity, thoughtfulness and prayerfulness. Christians differ among themselves as they seek to apply their faith in real situations in the modern world.

The view that the very earliest human embryos should be afforded the same degree of dignity and care as fully formed humans is argued by, among others, Philippa Taylor of CARE (2002) and by the pastor Brendan McCarthy in his book *Faith and Fertility* (1997). McCarthy concludes, as does the theologian Richard Hays (1996), that there are no proof texts concerning the status of the human embryo. Nevertheless, he extrapolates from the biblical references on God's care for the human growing in the womb to suggest that the early embryo should be afforded the same ethical status as the implanted embryo/foetus. Indeed, he suggests that it is Christians who hold other views (see below) who must justify their position. According to Christians who hold or who tend towards this view (and they include some medical practitioners and infertile couples), the early embryo should be treated as if invested with human personhood and with the image of God from the completion of fertilization, even if there is some uncertainty about the timing. It is, they argue, best to be cautious rather than unwittingly destroy another human being.

The view that pre-implantation embryos cannot be regarded as human persons has been presented by, among others, the consultant in medical genetics Caroline Berry (1993) and the embryologist (now science journalist) Peter Moore (2001). And this is the view that we, the authors of this book, also adopt. We do not take our view lightly. Many of those from whom we differ are acknowledged Christian teachers, who indeed over the years have been *our* teachers through their preaching and writing. Nor do we take the view that the pre-implantation embryo is just a blob of cells with which we may do as we please. It is human material that has the potential to become, through a long process of development, a human person. It is essential therefore that all work in this area is properly regulated, supervised and audited.

We hold this view for three main reasons. First, we accept the arguments from early embryonic development that the crucial stage biologically is implantation. It is this establishment of a relationship with the mother that permits the development of those embryos that actually implant. Further, the early embryo cannot be equated specifically with individual personhood, otherwise we would say that identical twins are half-persons and humans who are genetic mosaics are two persons.

Secondly, we believe that there is a danger of engaging in reverse transposition: that is, applying scientific knowledge to Scripture and then saying, 'Ah, that is what the Bible is referring to.' When we ask the question 'Did the biblical writers know anything about fertilization?' the answer is clearly 'No'. They knew nothing about human eggs produced by the woman. Indeed, the power of procreation was believed to reside entirely in the man, who contributed everything to the subsequent pregnancy. Male infertility was simply unknown and unthought of. Failure to have a child was always seen as the fault of the woman – she was 'barren'. The seminal fluid was the human seed and pregnancy was the fruit, not of fertilization, but of the womb in which the seed grew. Indeed, such views were prevalent for several more centuries.

What the biblical writers did know about, however, was not fertilization but conceiving a child. That obviously occurred after sexual intercourse, but it was only apparent when the woman missed her period and began to feel pregnant because of the hormonal changes going on. We suggest, therefore, that in the minds of the biblical writers human life began once a woman began to realize that she was pregnant. Indeed, biblical references to life before birth talk about growth in the womb and are thus dealing with pregnancy (growth in the womb does not occur until pregnancy is established). This happens as a result of implantation, and the woman's awareness of pregnancy occurs at this time or soon after. The biblical verses about growth in the womb cannot refer directly to pre-implantation embryos.

Thirdly, in Chapter 2 we referred to the process of decision-making that we believe is necessary in a fallen world. A number of ethical principles may have to be balanced in trying to make decisions. In this area we are concerned that an absolute prohibition on artificial reproductive techniques and embryo research, in our present state of knowledge, means that the suffering of infertility and of serious genetic disease will be unrelieved.

We believe that this principled pragmatism is a biblical application of the responsibility which Scripture places upon us: 'to act justly, to love mercy and to walk humbly with [our] God' (Mic. 6:8). It is justice and mercy that compel us to try to promote health and prevent suffering through these technologies. It is our desire to walk humbly with our God that compels us to try to understand what the Bible means by the 'image of God' and at what stage that applies in the prenatal development of human beings.

4. STEWARDSHIP OR DOMINION?

For since the creation of the world God's invisible qualities – his eternal power and divine nature – have been clearly seen, being understood from what has been made.
(Rom. 1:20)

There is something subjective, something philosophically naïve, and even something hazardous ... for humans to continue to live as though nature were valueless.
(Holmes Rolston) [1]

Introduction

It will be obvious from the previous chapter that humankind occupies a unique position within nature. Humans are part of the created order, a species within the wonderful biodiversity of the earth. We take our place in nature as mammals and, in particular, as primates. However, the differences between us and our nearest relatives (outlined in the previous chapter) also mean that we have extensive power over nature and can to a great extent isolate ourselves from it. But there is more: we actually exist on a higher plane than the rest of nature. We are made in the image of God; we have a spiritual dimension; we are able to relate to God. This places humankind in a position of special privilege, but also of special responsibility. How does this tension between privilege and responsibility work out? To try to answer that question, we now discuss attitudes to nature based on different world-views.

World-views and views of the world

Let us think back to those early humans that we referred to in the previous chapter. The world around them must have seemed a place

---

1. Rolston (1999), p. 361.

of contrasts: it provided them with the means of daily living in terms of food and material for shelter and, if need be, clothing. But it was also very threatening: some of the other inhabitants, the predacious animals, were clearly dangerous and care needed to be taken when away from suitable refuges; some of the plants made them ill and had to be avoided. Then there were those natural phenomena that seemingly came at random – storms, eruptions, even earthquakes. Early humans were also beginning to develop ideas about the possibility of a life beyond this one, a spirit life. Is it, then, any wonder that many 'primitive' cultures saw in nature the presence of spirits, either in the elements of nature themselves ('animism') or as beings that manipulated nature? Some spirits were benign but some were certainly malign, and in some cultures elaborate ceremonies of both celebration and appeasement (such as sacrifice, even human sacrifice) were developed. Even if nature was a provider, it could not be taken for granted. More advanced forms of this type of religion were seen in the Greek and Roman civilizations, in which a whole series of gods, often visualized as having human form, were responsible for particular aspects of existence (e.g. the god of war, or the goddess of healing) and certainly affected human affairs. This is of course in marked contrast to the biblical view of the one God, revealed to and in covenant relationship with humankind.

From ideas about spiritual beings indwelling or controlling nature it is easy to move to regarding nature itself as divine: that is, having the nature of a god. We see variants of this in eastern religions and in the traditional religion of Egypt. Elements of nature, particularly heavenly bodies and certain animals, were regarded as physical manifestations of gods (and in some eastern religions this is still so), and it is but a short step from there to regarding the whole of nature as divine. This is called pantheism ('god everywhere'). The idea of nature as being indwelt by gods or as being god also occurred in pre-Christian paganism in what is now northern and western Europe. Indeed, reminders of this religion are still seen in parts of northern Europe, from pub names such as Jack in the Green in the United Kingdom to sun and moon symbols in Lithuania. Further, there has been a resurgence of some of these ideas in the New Age movement, some adherents of which are clearly pagan ('neo-pagan') in their views of nature.

The Judaeo-Christian view does not ascribe divinity to nature, but regards nature as being the result of the activity of a single creator God who is outside nature but who sustains it in its continuing existence. It is significant here that the Hebrew Scriptures do not actually have a word that translates as 'nature'. They refer instead to 'the creation', focusing on nature as the work of God. Even in the Christian era, however, nature was still regarded on the whole as threatening and beyond human control. It was the advance of science in the seventeenth and eighteenth centuries that began to dispel this view. Many of the scientists at that time were Christians and believed that in their science they were observing the work of God. However, there were some people, such as Goethe, who looked back at the work of Francis Bacon[2] and Isaac Newton and worried that the systematic approach of scientists would take the mystery out of nature. Indeed, as science revealed a universe that behaved systematically and predictably, some thinkers came to view nature as a set of mechanisms.

In the Judaeo-Christian view, the creative work of God is a continuing activity. However, the idea of nature as a set of mechanisms began to exclude God from a continuing involvement in the running of the universe. God may be regarded as the original creator, but a creator who has, as it were, wound up a watch and is now letting it run. It is a short step from there to regarding nature as a sort of machine which is running according to the 'laws of nature', but without any external purpose or direction. Nature, including all living things, humans among them, is simply there; it is autonomous, free-standing and, in the very fact that it exists, mysterious. And that is the view held by many in the early twenty-first century.

The Judaeo-Christian view of creation

As we noted above, the Judaeo-Christian view of nature is that it is, in all its vastness, the work of the creator God who brought it into being from nothing and who continues to uphold and sustain it. Investigation of nature reveals some remarkable features. The precision of its 'foundational laws', the laws that govern nature's mechanisms, is one of these. John Polkinghorne (1998) describes how the extraordinarily precise working of these laws makes possible the existence of the

---

2. Francis Bacon was insistent that understanding God's creation in nature required evidence that could be gathered only by experiment, by careful measurement and by rigorous observation.

universe as we know it, from the establishment of the main gaseous composition of stars via the formation of carbon to the origin of carbon-based life. Further, the laws must have been working from the very moment at which God called forth creation out of nothing. The way the universe 'is' has thus made possible the development of life on earth in its present form. God has provided the exact conditions needed for the emergence of a particular kind of living being, humans, made in God's image for a relationship with him. This precision in the foundational laws has impressed many physical scientists, and some, like John Polkinghorne, have talked about the *anthropic principle*: that the foundational laws of the universe seem to be geared to allowing the emergence and the existence of humans (Polkinghorne, 1998: 36 et seq.). However, some biologists, such as Richard Dawkins, have poured scorn on this idea. In his obituary tribute to Douglas Adams, the author of the wonderful *Hitch-hiker's Guide to the Galaxy* (and the other four books in the trilogy – sic), Dawkins recalled how he and Adams had laughed at the idea, suggesting that it was like saying that a depression in the ground was exactly the right size for the puddle that filled it.[3] This is a misunderstanding of the anthropic principle. In such an illustration we would need to say that the depression in the ground had been made as preparation for collection of the exact amount of water (not one molecule more, not one molecule less) that would fill it. It would be a very precise puddle (although perhaps a rather weak illustration of the anthropic principle!). In contrast to the view expressed by Dawkins and Adams, many physicists, even those who do not speak from a position of faith, are genuinely amazed at the precision of the universe's foundational laws and the way in which their operation has led to life as it now exists. To paraphrase John Polkinghorne and the Australian astrophysicist Paul Davies, there is more going on here than meets the scientific eye.

Thus the Judaeo-Christian view sees nature as the ongoing work of God and its beauty and order as pointing to God. The psalmist declares (Ps. 19:1–2):

The heavens declare the glory of God;
    the skies proclaim the works of his hands.

---

3. Although this comment was made by Richard Dawkins in the original article in the *Guardian* (14 May 2001), it does not appear in the version published in the recent anthology of Dawkins' work, *A Devil's Chaplain* (2003: 165).

Day after day they pour forth speech;
    night after night they display knowledge.

Humankind has a special place in nature, being part of the created order but also the high point of God's creation, made for a relationship with him. As was noted at the start of the chapter, this is a position of great privilege but also of great responsibility, and it is the exercise of that responsibility that we now consider.

Stewardship or dominion?

In the first chapter of Genesis humankind is seen as being given dominion over the rest of creation (Gen. 1:28), and this theme is echoed elsewhere in Scripture, for example in Psalm 8. However, this view of humanity's relationship with nature has come in for some fierce criticism. In particular, it has been suggested that the Judaeo-Christian view has been at the heart of the ecological crisis of which we started to become aware in the 1960s. The historian Lynn White, for example, believed that the concept of dominion had placed humans at the centre of all things (the anthropocentric view of nature) and had given them *carte blanche* to do with nature as they pleased. This attitude, he suggested, had been the root of the ecological crisis (White, 1967). However, while it is undoubtedly true that human activity has been very damaging to the earth's ecosystems, it is not entirely accurate to ascribe this solely to the doctrine of dominion. In particular it ignores the element of stewardship that is built into the Hebrew word translated as 'dominion'. Thus David de Pomerai, a biologist who is also an Anglican minister, writes:

> The words of Genesis 1:28 take on an ominous ring when we consider how Western man has responded all too literally to God's commands to be 'fruitful and multiply' and to 'have dominion over . . . every living creature'. Entire ecosystems have been devastated in the name of Western progress, entailing forest destruction, decimation of dominant animals (such as bison) and massacres of indigenous peoples. More recently, we have added industrial pollution and intensive agriculture to the growing degradation . . . *The original sense of responsible steward-ship implicit in the Hebrew word for 'dominion' has become lost*

beneath a welter of profiteering and greed (de Pomeroi 2002; italics added).

These are strong words indeed, but they show clearly what happens when humankind first misunderstands the concept of dominion and secondly is, in any case, increasingly free from any idea of a creator God.

Further, the idea runs like a thread through the Scriptures that nature not only is the creation of God, but also belongs to God. If we Christians have taken a cavalier view of the world, it is because we have not taken seriously our responsibilities as stewards. If we have dominion, it is as if we are gardeners, caring for someone else's garden but allowed to use its resources. It is in this capacity that we must try to use the earth's resources wisely and with respect, acknowledging the work of God the creator and having care and compassion for our fellow human beings.[4] In other words, our view of nature should be *theocentric* rather than anthropocentric. It is in this light that we need to evaluate advances in science and technology; thus we now look briefly at science itself.

What about science?

In addition to their ability to manipulate nature, humans in general have both a curiosity about the world they live in and an inventive ingenuity that helps them to investigate nature and utilize its resources. Of course, these attributes are differently developed in different people, and furthermore ability to express them will be affected by circumstances. Nevertheless, it is this curiosity and ingenuity that have driven humans to investigate, with increasing levels of organization and sophistication, the universe in which they live. This is of course the practice of science, and in Chapter 1 we examined the limits of science in relation to the quest for religious truth. In this chapter we have reminded ourselves that, in the expansion of Western science that occurred after the Baconian

---

4. Readers wishing for a fuller treatment of these ideas are referred to the excellent briefings on the website of the John Ray Initiative (www.jri.org.uk) and to R. J. Berry's very useful book *The Care of Creation: Focusing Concern and Action* (ed. Berry, 2000).

revolution, many of the most prominent scientists were Christian believers. Indeed, Copernicus believed that gathering knowledge about the works of God through research was one of the highest forms of worship. We have also noted how modern research into the way the universe works is raising metaphysical questions and challenging some who hold a purely mechanistic view of the universe.

As science started to flourish, the whole of nature must have seemed open for investigation, from the movements of the planets and stars in the heavens to the functioning of plants and animals; indeed, the foundations of many aspects of modern science were laid in the eighteenth and nineteenth centuries. At no time did it appear that any area of investigation was felt to be unsuitable for a Christian believer (or indeed for a humanist). But today we hear suggestions from Christians, from other faith communities and from non-believers that some areas of research should be 'off limits'. The reason for saying this is usually that the potential applications of the knowledge are fraught with the danger that it will be misused. We will return to this shortly. However, some Christians have expressed more fundamental concerns of two types. First, the question is asked whether there are any areas of knowledge from which God has warned us away. We can see no biblical justification for such a view.[5] Rather, we see the exercise of God-given scientific curiosity as part of the stewardship of the earth that God has given to humankind.

Secondly, there is a growing anxiety about science, or even an antagonism to science, especially among some evangelical groups. There is a worry that the scientific enterprise itself may be biased against the Christian faith. As we have shown in Chapter 1, this fear is groundless. Although some scientists, such as Peter Atkins, Richard Dawkins and Francis Crick, have expressed strongly anti-religious views, they cannot ascribe these to their science or to the results it generates. 'Disproving' the existence of God is not part of science's agenda. And this leads on to the other aspect of current worries: that science may turn up something that is 'uncomfortable' or that makes me question my faith. Here we need to encourage. The searches for truth in religion and in science are, as discussed in Chapter 1,

---

5. It has been suggested that Psalm 139:6 is a prohibition of seeking some sorts of knowledge. We argue that the verse cannot be read in that way within its context. It is a lyrical expression of the feeling that everyone should have: that the ways of God can never be fully understood.

compatible with each other. Indeed, as the philosopher Roger Trigg has written in the context of a critique of postmodernism, 'science needs a metaphysical grounding if it is to be defensible. It can find this in the notion of an ordered Creation and a God-given rationality' (Trigg, 2003). In the same vein, the American theologian Ronald Cole-Turner (1995) states that 'religion gives science its purpose'. Science and religion are really partners! If we are keen to know the truth, then, we should not be afraid of what truth is discovered, in whatever field.

So we can see no limits to the subjects that science is permitted to research (and John Bryant has argued this case before: see Bryant, 1992). That does not mean to say, however, that all types of experiment are permissible; thus some areas will (and must) proceed more slowly than some scientists would like. Experiments that we regard as impermissible include those that degrade the environment and those that cause significant suffering to animals for relatively trivial results. Both of these examples relate to our role as stewards; the latter is also related to our modern understanding that higher animals can suffer both pain and stress. If animals are subjected to suffering, surely that should occur only in the service of significant alleviation of human suffering: for example, in the relief or prevention of disease. It would not, for example, include animals suffering for the sake of evaluating a new cosmetic. We also regard as impermissible any experimentation on humans without consent. Even with consent, some experiments must be regarded as unethical, such as attempts at directed breeding, which turns humans who engage in sexual union (and the resultant babies) into experimental subjects, will probably remove sexual union from the context of a committed, long-term loving relationship, and further has a strong eugenic subtext. Even if the selective breeding were undertaken via IVF (removing the act of physical sexual union), the eugenic subtext would still remain and one would be very concerned as to the motivation of the researchers. Readers will doubtless be able to add to this list, but none of these prohibitions refers to areas of knowledge, only to the means of acquiring it.

Applications of scientific research, however, are another matter altogether. The issue is not whether particular discoveries are morally wrong, but what human beings do with them. Because this is a fallen world where men and women pursue their own self-interest, all scientific developments have the potential not only to benefit humankind but also to promote evil. We have already seen that humankind has treated the earth in a cavalier way. Much of that maltreatment came from misdirected applications of scientific knowledge: applications without a sense of stewardship, using the technological power provided by scientific knowledge in an unrestrained way.

That brings us to biology and biomedical science in the late twentieth and early twenty-first centuries. We have already noted the excitement of modern biological discovery, but also that such knowledge may be dangerous, as capable of misuse. In applying it we must maintain a very strong consciousness of our creator God, a strong calling to stewardship of the creation and great awareness of the need for a biblically based neighbourliness to fellow humans. So let us try to work out these principles as, in the next five chapters, we consider genetics, genetic manipulation and cloning.

5. MOVING GENES

And what does the LORD require of you?
To act justly and to love mercy
   and to walk humbly with your God.
(Mic. 6:8)

Biotechnology presents us with a special moral dilemma, because
any reservations we may have about progress need to be tempered
with a recognition of its undisputed promise.
(Francis Fukuyama) [1]

Some history

The development of genetics illustrates the way that humankind's
God-given curiosity about nature has become formalized in science.
A brief history also provides essential background understanding
for the discussion of genetic modification and related topics in this
chapter and the next two. Ideas about the inheritance of physical
traits or characteristics go back a very long way. It is clear from
archaeo-botanical research that human communities in the Fertile
Crescent were applying selection to cereal crops probably as long
ago as 10,000 BC (Tudge, 1998), while in biblical records Jacob's
experiments with sheep (Gen. 30) suggest that he knew something
about animal breeding. Certainly both Hippocrates, writing in about
400 BC, and Aristotle (in about 350 BC) recognized that certain
physical characteristics ran in families; Aristotle also observed that
sometimes children can look more like their grandparents than their
parents. About 600 years later, as noted by Steve Jones (1996: 9), the
general understanding that traits run in human families was apparent
among Jewish scholars: in AD 200 Rabbi Judah the Patriarch granted
exemption from circumcision to other members (including cousins)
of families in which a baby boy had bled to death after being

---

1. Fukuyama (2002), p. 84.

circumcised (the first indication in the literature of a knowledge of haemophilia). By the nineteenth century this understanding of the inheritance of particular traits was becoming more formalized, with reliable observations on, for instance, the repeated occurrence of particular diseases within certain families (e.g. haemophilia among the relations of Queen Victoria) or the passage of flower colours from generation to generation.

The basis of these inheritance patterns was completely unknown. One idea was that these traits were 'in the blood'[2] of humans and other animals, and that in producing children the bloodlines of the parents were mingled together to give a sort of average. Of course, this did not explain why a child might inherit a specific feature from one parent rather than from the other; thus some traits were regarded as being stronger or more 'dominant' than others (a term still used in modern genetics). The idea of characters being 'in the blood' is of course long discarded, but the terminology remains with us when, for example, we describe racehorses as being of good blood stock.

Exactly how plants could pass on traits 'in the blood' was never made clear, but by the middle years of the nineteenth century results obtained by plant breeders were about to revolutionize our understanding of inheritance. The work of Goss in the 1820s, at Hatherleigh in Devon, was a particularly good example. He noted that, in peas, flower and seed colour usually did not 'average out' when crossings were performed but were passed on as distinct characters. Even more intriguing was his observation that some characters could be 'hidden' for a generation and then reappear in a subsequent cross. This was equivalent to that observation first made many centuries earlier that children may closely resemble their grandparents.

Thus we come to the Christian monk Gregor Mendel, working at Brno in Czechoslovakia. His experiments were similar to those of Goss, but he took them much further, in particular by carrying out a numerical analysis of the occurrence of each character in each generation of crosses. From his results, he formed the following conclusions. Inherited traits were determined by factors that must have a physical entity. (We now name these factors *genes*.) For a given character, such as seed colour or petal colour, the factors come in two

---

2. Steve Jones provides a fascinating commentary on the outworkings of this view in his book *In the Blood: God, Genes and Destiny* (Jones, 1996). Note that, despite the title, it is not written from a Christian standpoint.

Genetics: the background

- Evidence for crop selection goes back about 12,000 years.
- There were attempts at selective animal breeding in Old Testament times.
- In immediately pre-Christian times, Greek scientists developed the idea that traits ran in families.
- That idea was developed slowly in the Christian era.
- The work of the monk Gregor Mendel (carried out in the nineteenth century but rediscovered in 1900) showed that inheritance was based in physical entities that were passed on from generation to generation.
- Johanssen coined the word *gene* as a name for these inheritance factors.
- A gene can exist in more than one version.
- The different versions are called *alleles*.
- Humans (and many, many other living things) possess two sets of genes in all their cells except sperm and egg.
- For any one gene, we may have two copies of the same allele: in respect of that gene we are *homozygous* (Gk. *homo*, 'same').
- Or we have two different alleles: in respect of that gene we are *heterozygous* (Gk. *hetero*, 'different').
- Genes are associated together in groups that have a strong tendency to be inherited together; this is called *linkage*.
- Genes in different linkage groups act independently from one another in inheritance; this is called *independent segregation*.

different versions and one of these versions may be dominant over the other. (These versions are now called *alleles*.) In a normal mating, one parent contributes one set of factors and the other parent another set. For any particular factor the two parents may contribute the same version (allele) or different versions. In modern genetic terminology, the offspring will therefore be either *homozygous* (both copies the same) or *heterozygous* (two different versions). Finally, the factors determining different characters are independent of each other and can 'travel' separately in inheritance. Thus, for example, the factor (gene) determining pea-flower colour is separate from the factor determining the wrinkled or smooth character of the seed coat. In today's parlance, we speak of *independent segregation*.

Approaching an understanding of genes

At the time of its original publication, Mendel's work received little attention. It was its rediscovery in 1900 that was a major landmark in the development of genetics. It was quickly realized that the behaviour of chromosomes – coloured sausage-like (or sometimes thread-like) bodies seen in cells – observed under the microscope during the formation of gametes (sperm or eggs) was consistent with Mendel's hypothesis on the segregation of genes (to use current terminology). There must, however, be many more genes than there are chromosomes; thus the concept developed that genes were parts of chromosomes. Further studies of the inheritance of genes by means of crossing experiments showed that genes were in groups: different groups of genes did indeed travel separately, as described by Mendel, while genes within the same group behaved as if they were totally or partly linked together. In fact, the term *linkage* was adopted for this phenomenon, and it was established that the number of groups of linked genes was the same as the number of chromosomes observed with the microscope. A chromosome and a linkage group were thus the same thing. Analysis of the degree of linkage between genes enabled geneticists to build up maps of genes in relation to each other and thus to place genes in order along the chromosome. It must be emphasized, of course, that this type of mapping was confined to genes that had a clearly observable effect on the organism[3] and thus represented only a fraction of the genes possessed by that organism. Nevertheless, such mapping was an essential background to the genome projects described in Chapter 6.

So chromosomes are the entities that carry the genes, and genes are the factors that determine the possession of particular character-istics. But which components of the chromosomes are the genes? This problem was solved in 1944, when it was demonstrated unequivocally that it is the DNA (deoxyribonucleic acid) that carries genetic information. This is a long, thread-like chemical built up from four different building blocks (bases) that are joined together in a linear array which may number many hundreds of millions. In relation to chromosomes we can thus say that the linear array of genes in one chromosome represents a single thread-like molecule of DNA. The discovery that DNA, which had previously been thought of as being rather a dull chemical, is the genetic material led to a race to discover its structure. As is well known, the

---

3. Biologists speak of *genotype* to describe the suite of alleles possessed by an individual and *phenotype* to describe the outworking of the genotype in the individual.

race was won by Francis Crick and James Watson, but they could not have done so without the data provided by Rosalind Franklin and Maurice Wilkins. We note in passing that it remains a scandal that Rosalind Franklin's major role in this work was not properly acknowledged for many years[4] (although she was a co-author of one of the three papers published in that famous edition of the prestigious science journal *Nature*).[5]

The structure of DNA exhibits two features that are relevant here. First, the thread-like molecules are actually formed of two threads, wound round each other as in a rope – the famous *double helix*. Each can act as a template for building the other, thus preserving the genetic information from generation to generation. Secondly, in building each thread, the four bases (building blocks) may be placed in any order (see Figure 5.1a); thus in a long thread the number of possible combinations of bases is truly vast. This in turn means that the order of the bases in the DNA could contain the genetic information. This hypothesis was confirmed in the 1960s with the unravelling of the *genetic code* that resides in the bases. We may therefore regard a gene as a specific linear array of bases that gives a specific instruction to the cell. In effect, each gene is a recipe, with each component of the recipe being specified by three bases. The product of each gene, the outcome of the cell using the recipe, is a *protein* (see Figure 5.1b). Many tens of thousands of proteins are known in nature; these are the cell's working molecules, on which the structure and function of the cell directly or indirectly depend. One further and very important feature of the genetic code is that it is *universal*: all organisms use the same code. Thus, in reading genes, a particular array of three bases specifies the same recipe component (i.e. the same protein building block), whether the code is being read in an aardvark or an antirrhinum, a microbe or a mouse. *They all read the code the same way.* As is discussed later, this has significant implications for genetic modification.

We have built up a picture of a gene as being a particular tract of

---

4. Whether or not she would have shared in the Nobel Prize is a matter for conjecture since, sadly, she died before the prize was awarded for this work (Nobel Prizes are not awarded posthumously).

5. The three papers describing the structure of DNA, including that of Crick and Watson, were published on 25 April 1953. This page is being written exactly fifty years later!

(a) The code in DNA

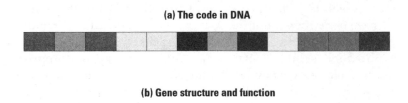

(b) Gene structure and function

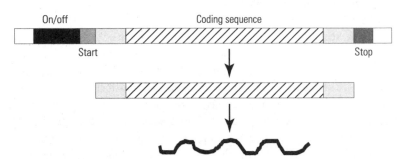

The gene, including the border non-coding sequences, is copied into a messenger molecule, effectively a working copy of the gene.

The 'recipe' in the coding region of the messenger is translated into a specific protein, one of the cell's 'working molecules'.

Figure 5.1. (a) A small part of a DNA strand in which the four building blocks (bases) are represented by four different shades; (b) 'Cartoon' of gene structure and function (not to scale)

DNA within a much longer DNA string, the chromosome. Within the gene, the order of the bases provides a 'recipe' for building one of the many proteins that a cell requires in order to function. We now need to add two more features in order to complete this basic picture. First, each gene has an on/off switch called a *promoter*, which controls the timing and (in organisms with more than one cell) the location within the body of the gene's activity. These promoters are also part of the DNA thread; they are usually directly adjacent to the gene that they control (see Figure 5.1b). Secondly, except in the tightly packed genomes[6] of some micro-organisms, genes are only rarely directly adjacent to one another. They are more usually spaced out along the

---

6. *Genome* is a rather loosely used term, generally meaning the 'total genetic complement' or 'total DNA complement' of an organism (species or individual), and in this case is being used to refer to the genetic complement as a physical entity.

DNA molecule, so that there is a large amount of DNA that is neither genes nor promoters.

The complexity of genes, and of all the mechanisms involved in their function and inheritance, induce wonder in those privileged to work in this area. One of us has been researching on the biochemistry of gene function and inheritance for over thirty years and is still amazed at the awesome beauty of it all. The psalmist looked to the heavens and saw God's glory (e.g. Pss. 8; 19). Today, we can still do that; but we can also see his glory in the living cell.

Genetic modification – the basics

Genetic modification (GM) dates back to the early 1970s; it depended for its invention first on a slowly growing knowledge of genes (based on painstaking biochemistry and genetics) and secondly, within that growing knowledge, on certain key discoveries made in the previous decade. These were:

- Bacteria (single-celled micro-organisms) repel invading viruses by cutting the virus DNA in specific places.
- All living cells possess mechanisms for rejoining broken DNA molecules.
- Bacteria possess, in addition to their main chromosome, small 'extra' bits of DNA containing only a few genes. These are called *plasmids* and in nature they are moveable between bacterial cells.
- The viruses that invade bacteria (known as *bacteriophage*), provided they evade the bacterial defences, are also agents of gene transfer.

These discoveries led to the development of the essential tools for genetic modification:

- Cutting and rejoining DNA molecules[7]
- Changing the suite of genes present in plasmids or bacterio-phage, e.g. by adding a new gene
- Transferring the recombinant plasmid or bacteriophage to bacterial cells

---

7. That is, recombining DNA molecules in new ways, hence the biologists' original term for these techniques: *recombinant DNA technology*.

Genetics 1944–1973

- **1944** DNA discovered to be the genetic material
- Led to concept of a gene as an individual section of a long DNA string
- The gene provides a specific 'instruction' to the cell
- Each long DNA string is equivalent to a *chromosome*
- Thus, in terms of genetic information, a chromosome is a long DNA string embodying many genes
- Genes on the same chromosome are linked together; genes on different chromosomes segregate independently (see 'Genetics: the background', p. 75)
- **1953** Structure of DNA discovered – the famous *double helix* – leading to an understanding of how genes work
- **1960**s Genetic code decoded
- **1973** Invention of recombinant DNA techniques (genetic engineering, genetic manipulation or genetic modification)

The process, shown diagrammatically in Figure 5.2, is thus dependent on *natural gene-transfer mechanisms*. Nevertheless, the range of genes that it is possible to transfer into bacterial cells is much wider than would occur in nature; this immediately raises ethical concerns about the applications of these techniques. We leave until the next section the debate about the possible intrinsic rightness or wrongness of GM itself. Here we raise the issues of safety and of possible misuse. In both these areas, the scientific community showed enough awareness, first, to call a temporary embargo on further experimentation and secondly, during that embargo, to devise safety and ethical guidelines for the performance of GM experiments and the use of GM techniques. These guidelines have formed the basis for regulatory frameworks across the world, and in many countries these frameworks are enforced by government agencies. In the UK, even the research use of GM within laboratories is subject to regulation by the Health and Safety Executive and that agency may inspect a laboratory at any time. Further, these government agencies are not toothless: laboratories may be closed, or at least prohibited from continuing GM work, and in both the UK and the USA scientists who have contravened regulations have been moved to other work or have even been dismissed from their posts. Thus, in respect of a technology about which there were initial uncertainties, society has taken steps to protect both human beings and the

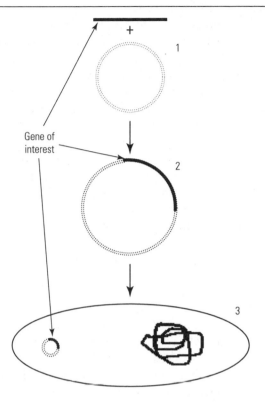

1. A gene of interest has been identified and isolated. Using biochemical tools (specific biocatalysts – enzymes), the gene is 'pasted' into a small circular piece of DNA known as a plasmid.

2. The plasmid now contains the gene of interest and, because it is a 'new' combination of DNA sequences, it is described as recombinant DNA.

3. The plasmid is then inserted into bacterial cells; if the inserted gene is associated with an appropriate promoter ('on/off switch') the bacterial cell will read the gene as if it were one of its own. If the foreign gene was the human gene that gives the instruction 'make insulin', then the bacterial cells will now make insulin.

    In the cartoon, the bacterium's main chromosome, a complex circular DNA molecule, is shown on the right. The cartoon is not to scale; in reality the plasmid is very much smaller than shown in comparison with the bacterium's main DNA molecule.

Figure 5.2. The essential features of genetic modification of bacteria

environment and to prevent the technology from being used against other humans. In the latter context, the regulations are strongly reinforced by international protocols prohibiting biological warfare. Now, while it may be a nuisance for a research-group leader, working on a topic that poses no environmental or health hazards, to conform to government-enforced guidelines, we suggest that Christians should welcome these regulatory frameworks. They represent a high regard for God's creation, a care for humans in general and a concern that God's good gifts in science and technology should not be misused. Thus, although GM is clearly one of those many areas for which there is no direct biblical guidance, we can apply the general biblical principles discussed in Chapters 2–4 above: love of God (Matt. 22:37), which includes respect and care for his creation (e.g. Ps. 104; Is. 48:12–13), and a neighbourly care for other humans (Matt. 22:39).

Once the regulatory frameworks were in place, the technique was very rapidly taken up by the pharmaceutical industry. This is exemplified by the deliberate transfer to bacteria of the human gene that normally instructs pancreas cells to make insulin (as in Figure 5.2), culminating in 1982 in the licensing for use in human therapy of insulin produced by genetically modified bacteria. As indicated earlier, it is the universal genetic language that makes this possible. The bacterium 'reads' the human gene as if it were one of its own and makes a product, i.e. a human hormone, that it has never made before. The fact that the insulin gene came from human DNA does not make the bacterium human. It is still very much a bacterium. This success has been followed by the production of many therapeutic proteins and of several vaccines in genetically modified bacteria and other micro-organisms. The technique has also been applied in the food industry. For example, it is used to produce an enzyme (biocatalyst) called chymosin for use in cheese-making, thereby avoiding the need to extract the enzyme from calves' stomachs. Cheese made in this way is sold as 'vegetarian cheese'.

Plant genetic modification

Introduction

We now turn to a topic that in recent years has been the subject of more general and prominent public debate than any other scientific or technological topic, more even than mammalian cloning (where the initial furore has died down to a background murmur with occasional louder rumblings). This prominence leads us to deal with the issue in some depth and at some length (but we provide a summary at the end of this chapter). It also leads us to suggest that Christians should be aware of it and, if appropriate, participate in the debate. Indeed, such an engagement is consistent with John Stott's call to 'double listening': listening to our culture in a way that is informed by listening to the Word (Stott, 1992: 94). Much of the debate has had a clear ethical dimension and Christians have been involved both as individuals and as members of Christian organizations. It has become a focus for many different concerns somewhat wider than GM itself, such as the effects of intensive agriculture on the environment and the role of 'big business' in agricultural developments. As Christians we can use this topic in our quest to derive ethical principles in areas where the Bible has little or no direct teaching. But in order to do this, we must first mention briefly the basic essentials of the science.

The basic mechanisms

The initial development of plant genetic modification also relied on *natural mechanisms*, and especially on the manner in which a particular bacterium, *Agrobacterium*, transfers some of its genes to plants. The details are not relevant for our current discussion, but readers who wish for a more extensive description are referred to Bruce and Horrocks (2001) or Hughes and Bryant (2002). We emphasize here that gene movements between species do occur in nature: the *Agrobacterium* system provides an obvious example. Furthermore, by study of this system biologists have identified the essential features of its gene transfer mechanism and have used them to transfer functional genes into plants.

This technique is both *precise* and *imprecise*. It is precise because, unlike plant-breeding techniques, one or a few specific genes, conferring desired characters, are transferred to a plant the rest of whose genetic characteristics are not altered. Thus specifically wanted genes can be moved into candidate varieties. This clearly contrasts with what happens in conventional breeding, where two complete sets of genes, albeit closely related, are mixed together and re-sorted, with a significant possibility of introducing unwanted characters into an elite crop line. However, genetic modification is imprecise because of *position effects*: there is no control over the place within the plant chromosome that the incoming genes are inserted into. This causes great variation from plant to plant in the first 'GM generation' in the extent to which the desired character is actually seen (in scientific terms, variation in the level of expression of the incoming gene). This means that there must be some selection of the first generation of GM plants, followed by observation of the stability of inheritance in subsequent generations. In practice, however, this phase is shorter than the 'sorting' and evaluation phase in conventional breeding, leading to a faster adoption of the new varieties. Thus the advantages of GM include the following:

- It enables the addition of specific genes to well-characterized varieties, including 'elite' lines.
- Those genes can come from widely separated species.
- New varieties may be more quickly adopted for use.

The main advantage of this technique, however, is that it increases hugely the genetic variety available to the plant breeder, while avoiding the problem of bringing in unwanted genes. Of immediate relevance to the grower is the ability to insert genes for resistance to pests and diseases; applications such as these are already in commercial use (but not, at the time of writing in the UK; a government decision is expected during 2004). Secondly, the ability to handle individual genes in the 'test tube' means that direct biochemical modification may be used to generate new variants in existing genes within a crop species. This leads us to explain that, although much has been made in some sections of the media of some examples of inter-species gene transfer ('fish genes in strawberries'), many applications of GM will involve transfer of individual genes between varieties of the same crop species, or increasing the number of copies of a gene within a crop variety, or switching off genes (as with the Flavr Savr® tomato), or even putting back a gene after it has been biochemically manipulated in the test tube. The distinction between 'conventional' plant-breeding and GM techniques is thus a very blurred one. Two further examples will help to illustrate this. First, short-stalked wheat was obtained by conventional breeding in the 1970s. However, the allele that causes the short stalk has now been identified, isolated and transferred to rice by GM techniques, without the problem of bringing in unwanted characters. Secondly, herbicide-tolerant oilseed rape has been obtained both in 'conventional' breeding programmes and by GM techniques. This example will be looked at again when we examine some of the objections to GM that have been raised.

Applications of plant genetic modification

In dealing with the actual and potential applications of plant GM we need to emphasize again a point made in the previous subsection, namely that many of the individual genes that will be transferred in these applications will not be crossing wide species barriers. We also need to distinguish clearly here between GM crops and GM foods. 'Vegetarian' cheese is clearly a food that is produced directly by a process that involves GM. Further, the component produced by GM, the chymosin enzyme, although used in the cheese production process, is to a large extent trapped in the cheese and thus also becomes part of the product. Turning to consider crop modification, we can separate those modifications that directly affect the food component of the crop (and thus may come within the category of GM foods) and those that affect plant characteristics that have nothing to do with the food component. In the GM food category, the slow-softening tomato, the first GM crop to come to market, is a clear example: the GM process affects the quality of the consumed product. There are other applications under development that also directly affect the food product. However, it is very likely that only a relatively small proportion of the modifications will directly affect the food component of the crop; many applications will enable the crop to resist pests and diseases or to withstand environmental stresses, while others will affect the way that a crop is grown. There are also several current applications using plants to produce non-food derivatives, including animal vaccines. Readers who are interested in further information on the range of current and possible future uses of crop GM technology are referred to a recent Evangelical Alliance report (Bruce and Horrocks, 2001). However, despite the wide range and actual or potential utility of these applications, there are many people, especially in the UK and in mainland Europe, who either object strongly to this technology or at the least have strong reservations about it. What then are these objections? Should Christians be especially concerned?

Questioning GM crops

Introduction

It is important for us to evaluate the objections that have been raised against GM crops. Some of these are specifically relevant for Christians, while others are of interest and/or relevance to all of society. Thus we will cover:

- Biblical perspectives
- Intrinsic deontological objections
- Risk and precaution
  - Food safety
  - Effects on biodiversity
  - Creation of 'superweeds'
  - Gene flow
- Risk, ethics and society
- Disadvantaging the poor

Before embarking on this analysis, however, we need to consider how the debate has been conducted in the United Kingdom over the past few years.

Conducting the debate

During the mid-1990s two GM food products were introduced successfully into the UK market. These were 'vegetarian' Cheddar cheese, and tomato paste made from the 'Flavr Savr'® tomato (in which the softening process had been delayed by inserting one of the tomato's own genes in reverse orientation). Although the latter initially attracted a low level of protest, both were quickly accepted by the public; indeed, in the two supermarket chains in which it was available the tomato paste achieved good market penetration. In 1999, however, the situation changed dramatically. The specific catalyst may well have been the importation from the USA of increasing amounts of soya products that carried no label to indicate that they were derived from GM plants. Indeed, under US regulations there was no need to label these products; the oil and the protein from the beans were not affected by the GM process and no plant DNA was present. To the campaigners, this lack of labelling appeared to be a means of circumventing consumer choice and thus forcing those with objections to GM to consume these products. This is particularly relevant in this example, because soya oil and/or protein are very widely used in the food industry.

We can speak from personal experience in saying that both the intensity and the breadth of the campaigning took the plant science community by surprise. We do not suppose that any of our readers has been called the 'Antichrist', as happened to one of the present authors in a public debate about GM crops! An accusation such as this obviously comes from deeply held personal views which were presumably at least partly based in religious belief. It also serves to illustrate the tone in which, sadly, much of the debate has been conducted, with little mutual respect between those on the opposing sides. This is in itself a serious matter for Christians; it is therefore relevant at this point to discuss the manner in which much of the debate has been conducted.

In his analysis of the GM debate, the sociologist Barry Barnes (2002) points out that, on the whole, the public have assumed that those who support the use of GM crops are biased but those who oppose the use of GM crops are unbiased, assumptions that he finds curious but which have nevertheless influenced the debate. It is thus all too common to be told that the scientists are all in the pay of interested parties, such as biotechnology companies, and thus represent the views of those companies rather than presenting 'objective' truth. This is an extension of the oft-repeated accusation that the biotechnology companies have lied to us about plant GM technology. Another symptom of this is that scientists are often accused of telling half-truths or even untruths in defence of a technology to which they have some sort of commitment (perhaps because they work on plant genes). Indeed, the very fact that one of the present authors works on plant genes and is, other things being equal, positively disposed towards GM as a tool for the plant-breeder may well cause some readers of this book to reject what we say here. Further, in Britain the GM debate has been conducted in the shadow of 'mad cow disease' (BSE), the outbreak of which many members of the public have blamed on scientists and especially on government-employed scientists. In any case, there is now in general much less trust of experts (see Barnes, 2002); this again makes it more likely that 'expert opinion' may be rejected.

Is there any basis in these accusations? Although most scientists are able to present views that are not determined by outside interests, it is sadly but probably true that, for the sake of effect, some scientists may exaggerate the significance of their findings or are inclined to gloss over problems. They may have a hidden agenda in that they have devoted many years of their career to this science and wish to see it widely applied. It is also certainly true that several biotechnology companies have made over-optimistic claims for the role of GM in feeding the world or for the potential benefits to consumers. More notoriously, one major company attempted to dress up advertisements as information briefings, a ploy that fooled very few people and led to even more distrust of the plant biotechnology industry. Further, in some instances the expertise of scientists and their commitment to the scientific method come over as arrogance or as an attitude of intellectual superiority. Scientists may label opponents of GM as ignorant, whereas many are well informed, with well-thought-out and coherent views. The wider public quite rightly takes exception to intellectual arrogance, and this may further strengthen opposition.

But what about the opponents of GM technology? Are they as unbiased and truthful as the public often assumes (see above)? Sadly, no. First, the opposition to GM crops, often outwardly based on environmental grounds, in several instances carries the hidden agenda of particular campaigners. For example, Lord Peter Melchett, formerly of Greenpeace but now linked with the Soil Association, has a personally held deontological objection to GM, stating that we know it is wrong and that we do not need these trials to show us that it is wrong (the trials being the UK farm-scale trials). George Monbiot, a regular writer in the *Guardian*, is among several people who oppose GM crops because they are part of the capitalist economic system and represent what is for this group the unacceptable role of 'big business' in agriculture and food production. Such hidden agendas were presumably behind the chopping down, in 2000, of many of the trees in a plot of GM poplars which could not pose any threat to the environment (female trees do not produce pollen and thus there could be no gene flow into the wild population). The trees had in fact been manipulated so that the wood could be processed for paper-making in a more environmentally friendly manner.[8]

Secondly, the campaigning organizations have also presented misleading and exaggerated claims, usually about the risks associated

---

8. One suspects that the motivation was an intrinsic objection to GM and/or an expression of opposition to the major company that sponsored the work.

with crop GM technology. The coining by several organizations of the term 'Frankenstein Foods' or 'Frankenfoods' and its release to the press was a master-stroke of misinformation, implying that GM represented the work of mad scientists and was likely to escape from their control. Further, the wearing of chemical protection suits in order to (illegally) tear up GM crops is tantamount to lying in that it implies that these plants are dangerous, indeed so dangerous that contact with them must be avoided. These impressions have been strengthened by a vigorous anti-GM-crops campaign in certain sections of the broadcast and print media, adding to public mistrust of the technology and of those who promote it. Indeed, on two occasions British juries have refused to convict persons caught and photographed in the act of tearing up GM crops being grown in farm-scale trials, on the grounds that those charged were doing a public good. Such has been the vigour of the campaigning against crop GM that it is hard to know what public attitudes would have been had the opposition been more moderate in style. The campaigners often repeat their claim that the British public do not want GM crops, but one wonders what the situation would have been had the campaigning been less strident.

What are Christians to make of all this? There are certainly Christians who work in the general area of plant genetics and some of these are directly involved with crop GM. As we noted in Chapter 4, we can see absolutely no inconsistency in this. There are also Christians who oppose the use of GM in crop breeding. As we suggested earlier, on issues for which the Bible provides no specific guidance different Christians may well reach different conclusions. Surely the important factor here is to act with integrity. Promulgating falsehoods about other's work is as much a contravention of the ninth commandment as is telling lies about those workers themselves. Making exaggerated claims of any sort, especially if others are misled, is equally wrong. We were therefore sorry to see that Christian Aid, which campaigns vigorously and with great impact about agricultural issues (including GM)[9] in relation to the poorer nations of the world, gave its support to a widely circulated leaflet that made misleading and erroneous statements about GM technology. This simply does not help. Let us attempt to conduct

9. Note that Christian Aid is strongly opposed to GM because of its potential for exploitation of the poor nations of the world: Simms (1999).

the debate with respect for those who hold different views and for the truth.

There are further challenges for Christians here. Of those who work specifically in crop GM research and development, or indeed in plant genetics in general, Perry (2003) asks, 'How does Jesus want me to react to those who vilify me, traduce me and trash my experiments?' Had we been the PhD student whose work was largely destroyed when the GM poplars were chopped down, how would we and how should we have reacted? Do we 'offer the other cheek' (Matt. 5:39), or is it acceptable to conduct a defence of our position? If, conversely, we believe that the use of GM technology is wrong, how will we behave if GM crops are introduced into British agriculture? How far should private morality influence public policy?[10] And for those on both sides of the debate, how will we work out in practice the exhortations of Paul: 'in humility consider others better than yourselves. Each of you should look not only to your own interests, but also to the interests of others' (Phil. 2:3–4)?

The Bible and plant GM technology

Are there biblically based objections to moving genes? It is obvious that if there are, they cannot be aimed specifically at GM because such techniques were undreamed of in biblical times. Thus, as we state several times in different places in this book, we can apply only general biblical principles to the issue. Space does not permit a lengthy discussion here. Readers who wish for a more in-depth analysis are referred to the Evangelical Alliance report *Modifying Creation?* (Bruce and Horrocks, 2001) and to the excellent and informative paper by Joe Perry (2003). Here we focus on two specific aspects of the topic:

- The question of 'kinds'
- The Old Testament laws concerning agriculture

It has been suggested that the movement of a gene or genes from one type of living organism to another offends against the concept of 'kind' (Gen. 1:11–12, 21, 24–25). Certainly, if species were fixed entities with clear boundaries between all species, such an argument

---

10. This question in examined in detail in Chapter 6, in the light of a specific case in human genetics.

might carry some weight and indeed might lead to a deontological prohibition based on the intrinsic nature of the 'kinds' of living organisms. However, it is clear from many years of biological research that species are not fixed, and that many of the supposed boundaries between species are actually rather blurred (see also Wright, 1989). Further, it is equally clear, as we have shown in the brief discussion in this chapter, that gene transfer occurs in nature, while study of genetics indicates strongly that in evolution genes may be transferred into an organism and become fixed into that organism's genome. If we are to raise theological objections to the very process of genetic modification, it is difficult to base them on the concept of fixed kinds, simply because such 'fixed kinds' do not exist.

Can we then find prohibitions based on Old Testament laws? Certainly there were laws that seem at first sight to be related to the issue. In Leviticus 19:19, for example, the children of Israel are commanded, 'Do not mate different kinds of animals. Do not plant your field with two kinds of seed.' However, these laws are usually interpreted as providing pictures within everyday life of the need for the people of Israel to keep themselves pure and separate from other races (see Bruce and Horrocks, 2001; Perry, 2003). These laws have certainly not presented problems for either Jewish or Christian plant-breeders who hybridize different plant varieties and species in the course of their work. It is thus difficult to prohibit the creation of GM crops on these grounds. Indeed, as pointed out by Perry (2003), modern Jews do not regard the use of food from GM crops as being contrary to their dietary laws; GM food may be as kosher as non-GM food. Christians are not of course bound by Jewish dietary laws, although Paul noted that this freedom must not be used as a total licence. Nevertheless, it is instructive to us to note that even strict kosher regulations do not prohibit the use of GM foods.

Are there intrinsic or deontological objections to plant GM technology?

A line of argument that clearly has some theological implications is based on the intrinsic value of the creation. We can identify three different reasons for ascribing an intrinsic value to nature. First, it may be regarded as being the work of God (the Christian, Jewish and Muslim view). Secondly, nature may be thought of as being in some sense itself divine, a view held by pantheists and by many pagans and neo-pagans. Thirdly, there are those who ascribe intrinsic value to nature 'because it is there'. The arguments raised by these different groups may well overlap somewhat, but the emphasis will differ between the groups.

In relation to the view that nature is the work of God, it often stated that moving genes between different organisms is contrary to the will of God, even an insult to God, because we are manipulating what he has created. In Britain, arguably the most famous statement of this position was made by Prince Charles,[11] who regarded the creation of GM crops as 'taking into the realm of man what properly belongs to God'. The problem with applying this view only to GM technology in relation to crops is that it completely ignores the myriad other ways in which humankind has modified God's creation by agriculture, medicine and many other spheres of activity. Further, many of those interventions are at least as dramatic as GM technology (and often more so), so it is hard to understand why GM in particular attracts this criticism.

In participating in the GM debate it has been a surprise to us that there are many people in Britain in the twenty-first century who hold a pagan, neo-pagan or even pantheist view of nature. It is presumably a reflection, first, of a thirst for spirituality that, sadly, has not been quenched by established religion, and secondly of the influence of 'New Age' thinking in this spiritual vacuum. The views of nature held by such people may be even more unorthodox if they incorporate into their thinking, consciously or unconsciously, some elements of eastern or native religions. One of the most vigorous proponents of this position in the GM debate has been the biophysicist Mae-Wan Ho. In a paper entitled 'Gaia and the Evolution of Coherence',[12] for example, she states: 'The Ufaina Indians in the Colombian Amazon believe in a vital force called fufaka which is present in all living beings.' The paper goes on to place modern research on biophysics, and particularly on bioluminescence, in the context of this 'remarkably coherent cosmology', this 'natural ecological wisdom'. According to this philosophy a gene is part of the wider web of nature, interconnected with the whole of the rest of the universe in such a way that moving it will disturb the distribution of the vital force. As Christians we must reject this view of nature (and be very careful that elements of it do not creep into our

---

11. Although we note that his Christian faith is far from orthodox.
12. The paper may be read at <www.i-sis.org.uk/gaia.php>.

thinking). It certainly does not provide any basis for raising intrinsic moral objections to GM technology.

The third group, who ascribe value to nature 'because it is there', often articulate their objections to GM as, 'It's not natural.' In doing so, they join many others who have no particular view on the value of nature but who clearly believe that, in relation to GM, natural equals good and unnatural equals bad. In essence this is the same argument, but from a non-religious perspective, as the argument based on interfering with God's creation. We (Bryant et al., 2002) and many others, both Christian and non-Christian, have argued that the distinction between natural and unnatural cannot be used as the main criterion in ethical decision-making and thus does not present us with any intrinsic objection to GM technology. However, we also need to point out that those who object to GM on this basis should also object to many other practices in plant breeding. These include:

- Achieving hybridizations between species that do not naturally interbreed.
- The use of radiation or chemicals to induce new mutations and thus generate more genetic variation from which to select. Several of the successful cereal varieties in the Green Revolution were obtained in this way, as was the barley variety 'Golden Promise', widely used in the UK brewing industry.
- The introgression into plant genomes of chromosome fragments from other species. In the 1960s and 1970s, before the advent of plant GM, British plant-breeders working at Cambridge produced high-yielding wheat varieties that carried a gene from a wild grass (to confer resistance to a particular disease) and a large segment of a rye chromosome.

Whether GM techniques are more or less 'unnatural' than these may well depend on one's preconceptions. For us, they serve to illustrate our view that GM is a very useful tool in the plant-breeder's armoury.

In reaching the conclusion that we can identify no theological, intrinsic or deontological objection to GM technology, we are in agreement with many other Christian writers who have considered the topic (e.g. Bruce and Horrocks, 2001; Deane-Drummond, 2001; Perry, 2003; see also the John Ray Initiative briefings by Berry and by Thompson: <www.jri.org.uk/brief/index.htm>). Nevertheless, we must accept that some people's views lead them to hold intrinsic objections to GM, and we therefore emphasize the importance of labelling of foods derived from GM crops.

We turn now to consider and analyse the specific questions that have been raised in relation to GM crops, attempting to deal with them from a Christian perspective.

Risk and precaution

Although we hold the view that there are no basic theological or deontological objections to crop GM technology, we nevertheless need to ask whether its use is too risky to be compatible with the concept of wise stewardship (see Chapter 4), or whether, because of risk, it represents an irresponsible exploitation of God's world. In order to set the scene for this discussion we now present some background information.

Plant GM was first developed in 1983 and by 1985 could be routinely achieved with several different plant species. By the end of 1985, plants resistant to the herbicide glyphosate (Roundup® or Tumbleweed®) had been produced by GM techniques and had even been subjected to small-scale field trials. Glyphosate-tolerant soya beans were first grown commercially on a large scale in the USA in 1996. Since then the area used for this crop in the USA has increased from the initial 1.7 million hectares to 34 million hectares in 2002 (reviewed by Perry, 2003). This represents about 70% of the American soya-bean crop.[13] On a world-wide basis, in 2002 some 53 million hectares were used for GM crops; these are mainly in the USA, but there are also significant areas in Argentina, Australia, Canada and China. The data from China are particularly interesting: of the 5 million farmers in the world currently growing GM crops, 75% are smallholders in China (Huang et al., 2002). Thus GM crops have been accepted in several countries as both safe and appropriate for farms of very different sizes and types.

A standard line of attack in campaigning against GM crops is that they are too risky. We examine this claim later in this section, but here we present one of the particular approaches taken specifically in relation to environmental risk, namely the *precautionary principle*. Widely publicized after the Rio Convention on Biodiversity, the principle states that we should not wait until there is scientific proof

---

13. Of the soya beans grown throughout the world in 2002, 50% were GM herbicide tolerant.

of (environmental) harm before acting to prevent that harm. As devised, it is strongly weighted in favour of those who, perceiving the *possibility* of harm, wish to take action. On this basis, some campaigners have opposed the UK farm-scale trials of GM crops on the grounds first that they are likely to cause harm and secondly that we do not need the data from the trials that are presumed to tell us this. The most extreme versions of the principle actually demand that a proposed new activity poses *no* risk. Bruce (2002a) refers to this as the 'hard version' of the precautionary principle. Thus one campaigning journalist wrote: 'When scientists say there is no evidence of risk we should be very wary; what is needed is evidence of no risk.' However, we may criticize this approach on the following grounds:

- All human activities carry risk of some sort.
- It is logically impossible to prove absence of risk: one of the first rules of scientific logic one learns is that 'one cannot prove a negative'. It is therefore difficult to know what is meant by 'evidence of no risk'.
- The application of the principle only to GM crops and not to other forms of farming is clearly a biased position. Logically, both conventional agriculture and organic farming, employing crops developed by 'conventional' plant breeding, should be subjected to the same precaution. After all, we have no reason to suppose that they are less risky than cultivation of GM crops (see also Perry, 2003, and Trewavas, 2001).

Confronted by the impossibility of meeting the requirements of the 'hard version' of the precautionary principle and noting the absence of application to conventional intensive agriculture, some have reacted by rejecting the precautionary principle entirely. Indeed, Bruce (2002a) suggests that this is now the prevailing attitude to GM in the USA agricultural industry. However, we hold that these criticisms of the way that the precautionary principle is being applied do not mean that we should ignore risk. Our care for the environment as stewards of God's creation and our love of our neighbour lead us to wish to expose neither to unjustifiable risks. Thus we now deal with the possible risks of GM crops, under four headings:

- Food safety
- Effects on biodiversity

- Creation of 'superweeds'
- Gene flow

Food safety

In the 1980s and 1990s Britain suffered a series of 'food scares'. These included the presence in eggs of pathogenic *Salmonella* and the transfer from beef to humans of a new form of BSE, known in humans as variant CJD.[14] Among the more risk-averse members of the British public there was a clear worry that much of our food was not safe to eat. It was no wonder, then, that when the public heard the term 'Frankenstein foods' (see subsection 'Conducting the debate' above), concern was further heightened that scientists might be 'meddling' with food in ways that might lead to further, as yet unknown, risks. Phrases such as 'supermarkets force-feeding us with the results of revolting genetic experiments' appeared in the press. As a sociologist of science, Barry Barnes, put it so well, the NGOs apparently campaigned on standard environmental grounds and yet the public were persuaded that GM foods were unsafe to eat (Barnes, 2002).

But is there a food-safety issue with GM crops? Our argument here, as elsewhere in this chapter, is that GM crops are no more and no less likely to be unsafe than conventionally bred crops. It is clearly illogical to suggest that a trait such as herbicide tolerance, if introduced by GM, presents a risk to food safety, while the same trait obtained by mutagenesis-based breeding (plant-breeding using new genetic variation that arises after deliberate creation of mutations) does not. The reality is that all new crop varieties, however produced, represent new combinations of genetic and hence biochemical activities. This was clearly illustrated when a new, conventionally bred variety of celery in the USA was shown, at a late stage of crop development, to cause an allergic reaction in a significant minority of people (Bruce and Horrocks, 2001). Neither parental strain showed this trait. Equally, it would be possible to transfer by GM techniques the gene encoding an allergenic nut protein to another food plant. The occurrence of such a protein in a foodstuff in which it was not expected would be very dangerous for those who are allergic to nuts. In this instance, it is good to know that, despite rumours to the contrary, such applications are not under development. Nevertheless,

---

14. Respectively, Bovine Spongiform Encephalopathy and Creutzfeld-Jacob Disease.

these examples demonstrate that growers and food producers have responsibility to evaluate all new varieties, GM or not, in relation to food safety. We also need to say, however, that even the most ardent anti-GM campaigners have been unable to detect any food-safety problem that is attributable to the GM crops currently in commercial use across the world.

Effects on biodiversity
Wherever humans have grown crops in an organized way they have attempted to reduce the biodiversity in the area in which the crops are grown: for example, in attempting to eliminate competing plant species – weeds – from the fields. Sometimes this proved difficult, as Jesus clearly knew in his telling of the parable of the wheat and the tares (Matt. 13:24–30). However, small-scale, non-mechanized farming, in which weed and pest control is very basic, does little to affect the overall biodiversity of a region, even in those places where the cultivable land is obtained by cutting down virgin forest (see Wright, 1989). Today, the situation is very different, particularly (but not exclusively) in the more economically developed countries. Much of arable agriculture is carried out on a large scale, with extensive plantings of individual crop varieties often covering many hectares. Cereal crops in particular have been selected for high yields, but in order to achieve those yields large applications of fertilizer are needed. Competition from other plants is reduced by applications of herbicides; for some crops, insect pests may need to be eliminated with insecticides. Control of many crop diseases has been achieved by intensive selective breeding, but for some diseases in some crops applications of fungicide are necessary. In some regions, even the seasonal pattern of planting has changed. In many parts of Britain, for instance, cereals and oil-seed rape may be sown in the autumn rather than the spring. It does not take much thought to suggest that modern intensive farming has, in the areas in which it is practised, reduced biodiversity; that suggestion has indeed been supported by several studies (see Perry, 2003, for a fuller account).

How do GM crops fit into this picture? Is there any direct danger that, by virtue of the crop itself or the way it is grown and managed, a GM crop will damage the environment and reduce biodiversity? There have certainly been reports that both insect-resistant and herbicide-tolerant GM crops may affect biodiversity: for example, by harming non-pest insects or by reducing food available for birds.

However, careful though much of this work was, it actually gave no indication of what happens in real agricultural situations, nor was any comparison made with the effects of normal agricultural practice. Readers wishing for further details of this debate are referred to reviews by Bruce and Horrocks (2001), Hughes and Bryant (2002) and Perry (2003). All these authors argued that GM crops did not pose any new threat to the environment or to biodiversity, although they acknowledged the reservations expressed by, among others, Sue Meyer of Genewatch (2002). Further information on GM crops and biodiversity were published in 2003 as the results of the farm-scale trials become available (see Perry, 2003),[15] although we note that some campaigning organizations have publicly stated, several months before the analysis was complete, that the results will be worthless. In the game of rugby such an approach is termed 'getting your retaliation in first'.

Creation of 'superweeds'

In a long study funded by the National Environment Research Council, it was clearly shown that agricultural crop plants are poor competitors in the field (Crawley et al., 1993, 2001). Although it is true that some species can grow as 'volunteers' in the natural environment, they do not become established as ongoing populations. Crop plants are strongly selected for performance in the very artificial environment of agriculture; in general, this makes them poor performers in the natural environment. The question then becomes whether a particular new trait, whether introduced by GM or by conventional breeding, will make a crop variety so competitive that it becomes a threat to native plant communities. So far, there is no indication of this (see Hails, 2000; Crawley et al., 2001; Perry, 2003), but that does not mean that it cannot happen. There is no reason, however, to suggest that GM per se is likely to lead to superweeds. The risk is related to particular genetic traits, not to the method by which those traits were introduced. However, we must remain aware of the possibility that gene flow from crops to wild species may transfer traits such as herbicide tolerance into the wild and therefore create a weed that is more difficult to control. Thus we now discuss gene flow.

---

15. *Philosophical Transactions of the Royal Society: Biological Sciences* vol. 358, no. 1439 (November 2003), was devoted to publishing the results from the farm-scale evaluations.

Gene flow

Gene flow refers to the movement of genes from one crop variety to another, or even from a crop to a wild species that is related to the crop. This can occur only if pollen from the particular crop variety fertilizes a plant of another variety or species. We must make the point that GM crops are no more and no less likely to outcross than are conventionally bred crops. There are very few crop species that are known to outcross readily with wild relatives in Britain, but two of them, beet and oil-seed rape, are among the crops for which GM techniques have been developed. However, in very extensive studies of hybrids between oil-seed rape and wild mustard species no evidence could be found for establishment of these hybrids. Nevertheless, again we must not assume that it will not happen. As discussed above, it will depend on the genetic traits of the crop and not on the method by which the crop was bred. We cannot say that pollen from GM crops will contaminate the natural environment while pollen from conventionally bred crops will not.

There is, however, one aspect of gene flow in which GM crops do differ from conventionally bred crops and that is in the flow to organically grown crops. In the UK, GM crops have been declared 'non-organic' by the organization that validates organic crops, the Soil Association. In our view, this is a difficult position to maintain in the light of the other methods that have been used to produce crop varieties that are approved. We also note that in the USA, where the organic agriculture movement is rather more diverse, some of the validating organizations have not accepted GM crops, but others have no problem in seeing them incorporated into organic husbandry. Be that as it may, it is clear that in the UK gene flow from, for example, GM maize to organic sweetcorn[16] growing nearby and downwind may pose problems. Although maize pollen loses viability very quickly, there is a real possibility that, at and near the downwind field margin, sweetcorn cobs will contain seeds that have arisen from pollination by the GM pollen. When crops are validated as organic, only a certain amount of 'contamination' from non-organic sources is permitted. It is thus theoretically possible that this limit may be exceeded, that validation will be withdrawn, and hence that the organic farmer will suffer financially. In the current situation,

---

16. Maize and sweetcorn are the same species; sweetcorn is a mutant that fails to turn much of its sugar into starch.

therefore, it is appropriate to take care in the location of GM crops in relation to organic farms if there is a danger of cross-pollination. This is showing love for neighbours by showing respect for their views and ensuring that they do not need to worry about validation of their crops.

Overall, therefore, we are of the opinion that it is not the method used to introduce a trait that should be evaluated for food and environmental risks but the trait itself. Indeed, the results of the farm-scale trials support this view. This will mean that a case-by-case approach needs to be taken to *all* new crop varieties, a suggestion that has also been made by other authors (e.g. Murray, 2003). This is the approach that Bruce (2002a) refers to as the 'moderate' application of the precautionary principle.

Risk, ethics and society

We cannot leave the subject of risk without a wider consideration in relation to people's value systems. As we have pointed out, all human activities carry risk and it is logically impossible to prove absence of risk. It is likely, however, that different people will find different risks and levels of risk differently acceptable. In respect of personal autonomy, risks that are chosen (for instance, in participating in dangerous sports) may be more acceptable than risks that are seen as being imposed (for example, in the production of staple foods). On occasions these choices may become confused, as when the siting of a mobile-phone mast is opposed on grounds of risk from microwave radiation, but the use of mobile phones is accepted as part of modern life. People may evaluate risks consequentially (albeit not necessarily consciously), by a personal cost–benefit analysis, in deciding which risks are acceptable to them. Further, one factor affecting that analysis may well be a person's value system. Thus, attitudes to risk have an ethical dimension (see also Bruce, 2002b). For this reason, there needs to be much more openness about all forms of agriculture, so that consumers know how their food has been produced. This is another reason for clear labelling of foods and agricultural produce.

There are some commentators, however, who take a less conciliatory line. Matt Ridley, a science journalist and author, says of the precautionary principle that it serves to maintain the status quo and ignores risks that are inherent in doing nothing, in refusing to move on (Ridley, 2001). In common with others (e.g. Perry, 2003), he suggests that the more affluent we become the more risk-averse we become (Ridley, 2003b). He urges us not to be afraid of science, but to recognize what a difference it has made to daily lives and thus to accept GM technology (and other recent developments) in the way that earlier scientific advances have been accepted.[17] He contrasts attitudes in the UK with those in the USA, where scientific advances are regarded much more positively and where GM crops have been used in agriculture for several years with no evidence of harm (note the careful wording). Ridley's comments have been publicly applauded by several scientists, including one distinguished Christian biologist; they have also, inevitably, attracted adverse comment from some anti-GM campaigners. Thus the debate goes on.

Bias against the poor?

As we discuss in detail in the next section, one clear aspect of GM technology is that it is mainly under the control of major commercial organizations in rich, developed countries. It is a powerful tool in the hands of the powerful. Several organizations, both secular (e.g. the Nuffield Council for Bioethics) and Christian (e.g. Christian Aid, the Evangelical Alliance, Tearfund), have pointed out that it raises the potential for further exploitation of poor nations by rich nations. Thus, in terms of world trade and in relation to its concern for the poor, Christian Aid has condemned the development of GM crops. In its report *Selling Suicide* (Simms, 1999) the possibility that GM technology may lead to further exploitation of the poor by the rich is clearly presented as making the technology irredeemable, so Christian Aid has proceeded to conduct a vigorous campaign against GM crops. We note that poverty is still a major factor in hunger and commend Christian Aid for its vigorous advocacy on behalf of the world's poor, for example, in the Jubilee 2000 campaign and in the current campaigning about the World Trade Organization. These activities very much reflect what Bishop David Sheppard called God's 'bias to the poor'. However, we do not believe that Christian Aid's campaign against GM crops per se is justified. Rather, we suggest that, if GM crops can contribute to food security in less-developed countries, we should campaign that the technology may be used with equity and with regard for global justice, rather than campaigning to

---

17. It is somewhat ironic that Ridley sometimes writes for the *Guardian*, a newspaper that has been consistent in its opposition to GM crops.

ban it. This approach has been adopted by Tearfund, which has a more evangelical constituency than Christian Aid. In its recent publication on GM crops Tearfund sees no inherent problem and thus gives cautious acceptance, provided that due care is given to ensure that the technology is not used in any way that exploits the world's poor or that is damaging to the environment. The Evangelical Alliance investigated GM crops and food from a rather broader perspective than either Christian Aid or Tearfund. Having examined issues ranging from scientific to theological, via environmental and sociological, the EA also concluded that there were no inherent objections to GM. However, their report (Bruce and Horrocks, 2001) again draws attention to the need to ensure that the technology is used with due attention to equity, global justice and concern for the hungry poor. There is thus absolutely no room for complacency; wherever possible, we should work to ensure that the economic and technological power of the developed countries is not used to disadvantage further the world's poor. So Celia Deane-Drummond (2001: 107) writes: 'We need to develop a deeper sensitivity to Wisdom's invitation to the banquet ... The figure of Wisdom is a reminder that our actions have to cohere with justice and goodness.'

Crop GM – the wider issues

Introduction
It will be apparent from our discussion about power and poverty in the preceding subsection that there is a range of wider issues to which GM crops have a relevance. Mostly, the relevance of GM is not specific but symptomatic of a more general situation. Nevertheless, these are issues about which there is concern and the relevance of GM as one of several contributing factors leads us to discuss them here. We do so under three headings:

- GM, world trade and less-developed countries
- Gene patents
- GM crops and 'sustainability'

GM, world trade and less-developed countries
The potential for GM to be yet another means of the rich exploiting the poor was presented above in the subsection 'Bias against the

poor?' We suggested there that, despite this, crop GM technology also had a potential for good in both poorer and richer nations. Exploitation of the poor is not built into the technology. However, we now need to discuss this issue in a little more depth.[18]

The Director of the Rockefeller Foundation, Gordon Conway, has stated that we need a new Green Revolution, a 'doubly green' revolution (Conway, 1997, 2000). He bases his statement on the prediction that in the next twenty years the human population of the earth will outstrip our capacity to produce food. He points out that the original Green Revolution in the 1970s came about because of a concerted and focused effort to increase the yields of cereals across the world. Further, although he does not see crop GM as a panacea for world food shortage, he does regard it as an important tool in breeding programmes which can thus make a significant contribution in increasing food production. With our Christian mandate to feed the hungry, should we then endorse Conway's views?

We need to look beneath the surface of Conway's statement. First, the Green Revolution is not without its critics. Certainly the new high-yielding varieties did well in South America and in parts of Asia: India, for example, became a net exporter of rice. However, high yields required high inputs; thus some less-developed countries became dependent on import of fertilizers from more-developed countries. Further, the Green Revolution did not help in Africa, where it was not compatible with local agricultural practice; nor did it utilize local indigenous knowledge (see Bharathan et al., 2002, for a fuller discussion of this).

Secondly, there is one major difference between the Green Revolution and the development of GM crops. The research for the Green Revolution and its subsequent application was largely implemented by government-funded laboratories and agencies, by charities and by international non-profit organizations. The bulk of crop GM research and development in the rich countries of the world is mostly carried out by large transnational companies. Indeed, as has been previously stated (Bharathan et al., 2002), the majority of the research and the resultant knowledge is in the hands of six companies or conglomerates. While we do not condemn the profit motive per se, it is difficult to see how organizations whose primary function is to

---

18. See also the extensive review by Bharathan et al. (2002).

make money can contribute to the application of GM to plant-breeding programmes for less-developed countries. In fact, the situation may be worse than this: the activities of the World Trade Organization, although ostensibly aimed at ensuring fair trade across the globe, actually favour the wealthy countries of the world.

These factors, combined with commercial practices adopted by some of the transnational companies, have led to suggestions that at present crop GM technology is a powerful tool in the hands of the already economically powerful that may all too readily be used to exploit the poor and the weak. Further, if anyone is in any doubt about the economic might of transnational companies, with their power bases in the world's richest countries, they should look at the way in which sugar companies have opposed the World Health Organization in respect of recommendations about the amount of sugar in a healthy diet. We are talking here not about the sugar-growers in poorer countries but about the sugar-refiners and processors, major food companies with extensive vested interests in increasing sugar consumption (interests which, sadly, do not include the welfare of West Indian sugar-farmers). Then there has been the battle about generic drugs for use in less-developed countries. Although the situation is improving slightly, it is very difficult to persuade some of the large pharmaceutical companies to relinquish their intellectual property rights over some patented drugs. The words of Amos ring loud and clear (8:4):

> Hear this, you who trample the needy
>   and do away with the poor of the land.

All this being said, it is clear that agricultural scientists and policy-makers in several less-developed countries see GM technology, appropriately applied, as a useful tool in breeding crops for their needs (reviewed by the Nuffield Council on Bioethics, 1999, and by Bharathan et al., 2002). Is there a way forward that does not involve further dependency or exploitation? This is a complex issue and space does not permit a full treatment here. In both the reviews cited immediately above, however, it is suggested that partnering arrangements between less-developed countries and international agencies such as the UN Food and Agriculture Organization and international non-profit organizations may be effective in aiding the less-developed countries to introduce GM into their agriculture without exploitation by powerful commercial interests in the richer countries. The development of 'Golden Rice'^{TM}, a rice genetically modified to increase its Vitamin A content, may be cited as a model for this approach.

Gene patents

One of the more contentious issues that has arisen in relation to the commercial use of GM crops is the patenting of genes. We deal with this topic in more detail in Chapter 6, in relation to human genes and their use in clinical diagnosis. Here, we need to point out that the registration of a gene as intellectual property contravenes one of the requirements for a patent to be granted: namely that the subject of the patent is an invention. No amount of argument will convince us that a gene is not a natural object, part of God's creation, which therefore should not be patentable (see Chapter 6 and Chapman, 2002). Further, the protection of genes as intellectual property is clearly much more restrictive than registration of a GM crop as a new variety under the Plant Variety Rights arrangements (see Hughes, 2002). Patenting of plant genes thus has the potential to increase further the power of the rich to the detriment of the poor.

There are some, however, who have argued that patenting of plant genes is a legitimate extension of international patent arrangements. Surprisingly, one such is Hughes, who, through his work with CAMBIA,[19] is clearly concerned that GM technology should be available to less-developed countries without exploitation by richer countries. He shows (Hughes, 2002) that although several patents stood in the way of the development of Golden Rice^{TM} (see above) it proved possible to negotiate, without cost, 'freedom to operate' (FTO) agreements in all those instances where a patent would have otherwise proved restrictive. However, this case is a very prominent one and it is highly likely that free negotiation of FTO agreements would be seen as showing the owners of the patents (the biotechnology companies) in a good light. There is no guarantee that future developments that are relevant to less-developed countries will be treated in the same way. In any case, the fact that FTO agreements were negotiated does nothing to change our view that genes should not be patented.

---

19. CAMBIA: Centre for the Application of Molecular Biology to International Agriculture (see Bharathan et al., 2002, and Hughes, 2002).

GM crops and 'sustainability'

In the UK, the results from the farm-scale trials were published in late 2003. One of the more interesting effects of the trials is that there has been more awareness of the impacts of 'conventional' agricultural practices on the environment and on biodiversity. As we have also noted earlier, it has been the practice of farmers from the very earliest days of agriculture to eliminate as far as possible any competing organisms and to maximize crop yields. There is a world of difference, however, between a small hand-weeded plot on which is grown a manure-fed or compost-fed crop, and scores of hectares of a single crop variety, treated with pesticides and herbicides and supplemented with inorganic fertilizers.[20] Thus, during a recent discussion forum at the Royal Society of Arts (see Christoforou, 2003), several contributors spoke of the effects of several decades of intensive agriculture. Over a period of forty years or so, wheat yields have increased several-fold; much of this increase is because of the efforts of plant-breeders, but those efforts would not have been so effective without an intensive cultivation system. Combined with changes in planting times, the effects of this on the environment are indeed becoming clear. Faced with this, there are calls for more sustainable farming: farming that requires less chemical input, that does not pollute the surrounding land and that is more 'in harmony' with the environment (without any clear definition of what 'in harmony' might mean, given that, as already mentioned, a farm, even an organic farm, *cannot* be a 'natural' ecosystem).

We also need to note, however, that, in respect of our food supply, the effects of our agricultural system have been very beneficial. The Evangelical Alliance report *Modifying Creation?* noted that the affordability of 'our daily bread' owed much to post-war plant-breeding and agricultural practice (Bruce and Horrocks, 2001). We must not be mealy-mouthed about this. It is one thing to be concerned about the effects of intensive agriculture on the environment, but quite another to suggest that in order to farm 'more sustainably' we must tolerate significant increases in prices of staple foods. This may be acceptable for those who enjoy financial security, but may spell disaster for those on low incomes.

---

20. The word *inorganic* is used here in its correct chemical sense; we are not contrasting it with so-called 'organic' agriculture.

So we have a quandary. We have a Christian duty to care for God's creation, which includes farming responsibly. In biblical times this was illustrated by the concepts of sabbath years and jubilee (Lev. 25), which emphasized that the productivity of the land could not be taken for granted; it was a gift from God. Therefore the land was not to be over-exploited. Today, our responsibility includes farming as sustainably as possible, avoiding pollution by non-benign or non-biodegradable agrochemicals, and preventing the run-off into watercourses of excess nitrogenous fertilizers. Yet we also have a responsibility to the poor that includes ensuring an affordable food supply.

To suggest that GM may have a role in helping us to farm more sustainably would to some people be total nonsense. They see GM as part of the intensive, science-based, 'reductionist' approach to farming which they are trying to replace with a less interventionist, less intensive, more 'holistic' approach. Yet the suggestion has been made by, among several others, Dr Brian Johnson of English Nature (see Christoforou, 2003). Is it really feasible? We must first note that many genetic modifications affect the crops of intensive agriculture and, unless a particular modification has an effect on the way the crop is grown, it is unlikely to contribute to increased sustainability. However, the applications of GM currently in use include herbicide tolerance, resistance to predation by insects and resistance to certain diseases. Disease- and insect-resistant crops need less application of pesticides and fungicides and so could contribute to a more environmentally friendly agriculture (but see the comments on bio-diversity under 'Risk and precaution' above). But surely herbicide-tolerant crops cannot contribute to sustainability? Certainly it might be expected that such crops would be treated with greater amounts of herbicide. Contrary to our expectations, this has turned out not be true, at least for glyphosate-tolerant soya bean; in this crop the total amount of herbicide used is less than for conventional varieties and the herbicide used, glyphosate, is more benign than that used with non-GM soya. Overall, according to a recent report by an independent charity that covered the seven GM crops grown in the USA in 2001, 20,000 fewer tonnes of agrochemicals were used in achieving a yield 7% greater than for equivalent non-GM varieties (American Society of Plant Biologists, 2002).

However, the concept of sustainability is rather wider than this. It involves land usage, application of nutrients to the land and – what will probably become the most important factor of all – water usage. Certain crops, such as cotton, are particularly 'thirsty', but across the world a very high proportion of all crops requires irrigation. Thus among the 'wish-lists' of farmers, and hence among the objectives of plant-breeders, are the ability to grow on more marginal land, better extraction of nutrients from the environment, and greater water-use efficiency. The analysis of plant genomes (see Chapter 6) may assist in identifying genes that contribute to these traits, thus facilitating the use of GM techniques by plant-breeders to introduce the traits into appropriate crop species. So GM could contribute to more sustainable farming, but it would depend on the motivation and funding of those who are developing these techniques.

Overview and summary

The topic of crop GM has been considered at length because of the continuing debate, much of it fierce and highly polarized, that it generates. At this point a summary will be useful in helping to identify the main points of the discussion, which we see as follows.

History
1. Plant GM was first developed in 1983, using a modification of a natural system that transfers genes to plant cells. Techniques have since been extensively refined, as a result of what has been learned about the natural gene transfer mechanisms. The main advantages of the technique are, first, that it allows the delivery of specific genes into elite crop lines, and secondly, that those genes can, if appropriate, come from a wide range of organisms.

2. After a period of extensive development, including controlled field trials, GM crops came to market in the mid-1990s. The first GM crops to be grown commercially were tomato and soya bean; since then, about six other GM crops have been added to the list. GM soya is the most extensively grown, with millions of hectares across the world. However, in the UK and in most other EU countries commercial growth of GM crops is not permitted. The UK government will make a decision on this in 2004, after the analysis of data from farm-scale trials.

3. Although purée from GM tomatoes had been introduced successfully into the UK market, the increasing penetration of the

British (and mainland European) markets by GM soya and products derived therefrom led to a widespread and concerted campaign against GM crops in general. The organizations conducting the campaign used the media very skilfully and enjoyed success in turning the British public against what are loosely called GM crops and food. Many aspects of the debate became acrimonious; one of the first casualties of war was truth, a situation for which both sides must bear some responsibility.

The current debate

1. Most scientists regard GM as a useful addition to the range of techniques available to the plant-breeder; many of the existing techniques already allow the creation of hybrids that cannot occur in nature.

2. However, GM technology is regarded as so novel that it requires specific evaluation.

3. There is no specific biblical guidance about GM. Further, we can find no general biblical principles that would lead to a prohibition of GM crops.

4. There are, however, some participants in the debate who, for various reasons, clearly have an intrinsic or deontological objection to plant GM technology. This view must be respected but, equally, those who hold it should make their position clear.

5. In respect of risk assessment we must acknowledge the personal ethical dimension: what may be acceptable to one person may be unacceptable to another.

6. Nevertheless, when GM technology is assessed alongside conventional agriculture we cannot see that GM per se poses any new risks that are not already posed by intensive cultivation of 'conventionally' bred crops in respect of food safety, biodiversity, the possibility of 'superweeds', or gene flow.

7. These conclusions do not lead to complacency. We suggest that both conventionally bred crops grown in intensive agriculture and 'organic' crops should be subject to the same scrutiny that is applied to GM crops. So it is again emphasized that *we should be evaluating the genetic traits themselves, not the means by which they were generated.*

8. We recognize that this may result in the rejection of some GM crop lines and – equally possibly – of some conventionally bred crops.

Wider issues

1. There are, however, wider non-technical issues that are of great concern. The main one is that crop GM technology is, with the exception of that being developed in China, almost entirely in the hands of major commercial organizations in rich countries in the developed world.

2. This, coupled with the way in which the World Trade Organization operates, means that crop GM technology may be just one more way in which the economically strong dominate and even exploit the economically weak.

3. A further factor is gene patenting. Although genes are not inventions, patent jurisdictions have been all too ready to grant patents on gene sequences. We believe this is wrong for two reasons: it claims that part of God's creation is a human invention, and it increases further the power of the rich over the poor.

4. The final area for discussion is sustainability. Intensive agriculture, which in Britain has contributed to the ready and affordable availability of our daily bread, has had effects on the landscape, the land and wildlife.

5. A very clear outcome of the farm-scale trials of GM crops, taken with other recent surveys, is that these effects of our agricultural systems are themselves now appreciated.

6. No farm, whether intensive or 'organic', is a natural ecosystem; indeed, in order to achieve good yields, both organic and intensive farmers must ensure that their crops compete successfully with the various organisms in the local natural ecosystem.

7. There is now a move to farm with an eye to sustainability – to minimize as far as possible the effects on the environment.

8. It has been suggested that GM technology may help to promote sustainability by producing strains that require less 'chemical support', for instance because they are resistant to predation by insects.

9. Others, however, have argued that GM crops are part of the intensive high-technology approach to agriculture and therefore cannot contribute to sustainability.

Conclusion

Even in this summary we can see that GM crops are a complex issue in themselves and that they also raise wider issues of great concern. Anyone who wishes to be involved in this debate (and we hope that many Christians would be interested in doing so) needs to be informed. Within the context of the debate we need to maintain respect for those who hold different views from our own. The words of James and of Micah set our standards here, both for our attitudes to one another and for our concern for appropriate application of the technology. We therefore end this long chapter with their calls to godly living.

> But the wisdom that comes from heaven is first of all pure, then peace-loving, considerate, submissive, full of mercy and good fruit, impartial and sincere.
> (Jas. 3:17)

> And what does the LORD require of you?
> To act justly, to love mercy
>   and to walk humbly with your God.
> (Mic. 6:8)

6. INVESTIGATING GENOMES

But the wisdom that comes from heaven is first of all pure, then
peace-loving, considerate, submissive, full of mercy and good fruit,
impartial and sincere.
(Jas. 3:17)

We hold these truths to be self-evident: that all men are created
equal...
(Thomas Jefferson: US Declaration of Independence, 4 July 1776)

Introduction

The development in the early 1970s of genetic modification techniques led to an expanding range of uses in altering the genetic
make-up first of micro-organisms and then of animals and plants.[1]
The extension of genetic modification (GM) techniques to 'higher'
organisms was predicted in the mid-1970s by John Bryant (1976)
and by many other authors. What many of us failed to appreciate at
that time, however, was the effect that GM techniques would have on
research. This is not the place to describe in detail the technical
reasons for this; suffice it to say that the extent of knowledge and
understanding of gene structure, function and organization in the
early twenty-first century was unimaginable only thirty years ago.
Investigations that had previously been carried out with great
difficulty, or regarded as impossible, are now routine.

One clear example of this is our ability to 'sequence' a whole
genome (an organism's complete complement of DNA). The amount
of DNA in the genomes of higher organisms is amazing. Indeed, to
Christians working in this area the structure and functioning of
genomes are further reminders of the awesome skill of the Creator, as
inspiring as the heavens were to the psalmist (cf. Ps. 19:1–4). Each

---

1. Although we have chosen to discuss plants before animals, techniques for
animal GM were developed before those for plant GM.

set of human chromosomes contains 3,000 million individual DNA building-blocks, arranged as twenty-three chromosomes.[2] Many plants have even bigger genomes. No wonder then that, prior to the application of GM techniques to research on genes, the very idea of determining the order of the bases in all the chromosomes of an organism was no more than a pipe dream. Thus in 1976 John Bryant wrote (p. 8):

> Because of the large amount of DNA in a plant cell nucleus it is impossible to determine the precise base sequence of the DNA. Even if the base sequence could be analysed at the improbable rate of one base per second, it would take ... years ... to complete the analysis.

How wrong one can be! Isolating and sequencing individual genes now form a routine research procedure. Analysis of whole genomes is rather more complex, requiring the coordination of work in several laboratories; it is nevertheless now part of the continuing research effort of the biological and biomedical science 'communities'.

The genome projects

This ability to determine the order of the building-blocks – the base sequence – of large amounts of DNA led, as just described, to a hugely increased level of activity in sequencing genes (and regulatory DNA regions such as gene promoters: see Chapter 5). The particular genes and other DNA regions to be sequenced, and the types of living organisms from which the DNA was obtained, were chosen to suit the research programmes of each laboratory. This resulted in a piecemeal approach to the analysis of individual genomes; thus the concept grew in the late 1980s and early 1990s of setting up international, coordinated genome-oriented research programmes. Sequencing programmes and problem-oriented programmes thus ran side by side. The best-known of these is the Human Genome Project (HGP), which we discuss in more detail later, but there are several others. Research programmes varied from those producing general

---

2. Our body (somatic) cells each contain two sets of twenty-three chromosomes; our gametes (sperm or eggs) each contain one such set.

information to others concerned with disease-causing organisms such as the malaria parasite, or with economically important crops like rice. In addition to these major tasks, some researchers undertake to analyse and map the many types of non-coding DNA that occur in nearly all organisms.

Progress has been unexpectedly rapid, not only in relation to the HGP but also in other organisms. New genome sequences are being published regularly. For instance, in the nine weeks between early October and early December 2002, two more complete genome sequences were published: those of the mouse (reviewed by Bradley, 2002, and Boguski, 2002) and the malaria parasite (reviewed by Doolittle, 2002, and Wirth, 2002). Earlier in the year, a 'first draft' of the rice genome had been published (see commentaries by Bevan, 2002, and Butler, 2002). Writing as a biological and a medical scientist respectively, we regard this as impressive – the 'wow factor' of Chapter 2 – and thank God for the gifts and abilities that he has bestowed, Impressive as this is, however, a genome sequence is just the end of the beginning: it provides a much stronger platform for research on gene function and gene malfunction (see Collins, 1999b).

Although we, in common with many others, in general approve of genome research, that approval is by no means universal. For some, this approach to genes – even the genes of non-human organisms – is dangerous, because it increases humankind's ability to manipulate nature (see also Chapter 5). Thus the theologian Peter Scott, writing about the HGP, states that it would have been better had it not been done (Scott, 2003). He is declaring this area of knowledge out of bounds for several reasons, including the danger that the focus on genes gives too much weight to our physical make-up and not enough to our spiritual make-up.

However, condemnation of the HGP is probably the exception rather than the rule among theologians (see for example Deane-Drummond, 2003), although discussion about the wisdom of pursuing the project continues. The science journalist Tom Wilkie, while generally supportive of such research, writes in his book *Perilous Knowledge* (Wilkie, 1994) about the dangers of misuse of genetic knowledge. Peter Moore, a science journalist writing from a Christian standpoint, uses the analogy of the Tower of Babel in Genesis 11:1–9 (Moore, 2001). In this story, humans had become arrogant about their own abilities; in order to 'make a name for

[them]selves', they decided to build a tower to reach the very heavens. Moore suggests that such arrogance may exist today within the scientific community, as it reaches out for the goal of understanding what it regards as the fundamentals of life. There is undoubtedly some truth in this suggestion, but also to be found are awe at the beauty of it all and humility in contemplation of life's complexities.

Further, for Christian (and indeed Jewish) believers engaged in this work, such hubris is quickly dispelled by reading those wonderful chapters at the end of the book of Job (38 – 41), where the story describes God as speaking to Job from the midst of a storm, asking him how much he has contributed to the creation: 'Who has let the wild ass go free? ... Do you give the horse its might? ... Is it by your wisdom that the hawk soars?' (NRSV). These passages remind Job – and us – of the might, power, creativity and wisdom of the living God. However much we discover about the workings of genes, the Christian response is that of Job: 'I am of small account' (Job 40:4, NRSV). In research, we simply have the privilege of 'thinking God's thoughts after him'; we should do so in thankful humility.

Genetics and eugenics

In the minds of many people, the very term 'human genetics' is closely associated with eugenics. There are worries that genetic selection and genetic modification may be used in a way that discriminates against some and favours others, in the name of societal 'improvement'. Although there is not necessarily a direct connection between knowledge of human genetics and actual eugenic practices, it is certainly appropriate to remind ourselves here of the history of the eugenic movement. As the philosopher George Santayana has put it, 'Those who cannot remember the past are condemned to repeat it.' That is not to say that we should go through life with our eyes constantly on the rear-view mirror, but it is clear that individual humans and society at large should learn from past experience, both positive and negative. In specifically Christian terms, we need to grow in discernment under the influence of the Holy Spirit, seeking to use God's gifts of scientific knowledge in a way that honours him.

The term 'eugenics' may be approximately understood as 'well-born' or 'good breeding'; its application to human society was first proposed formally in 1883 by Francis Galton, a cousin of Charles Darwin.[3] Galton applied Darwin's evolutionary theory to humankind by suggesting that the quality of the human species could be improved if those with 'better' qualities produced more offspring than those with 'inferior' qualities. Among the latter he included the 'criminal classes' (the 'morally incompetent') and those whom we would now classify as having various grades of learning difficulties (the 'feeble-minded'). Although support for such views declined in the UK after the Second World War, there was still an identifiable eugenic movement, albeit much reduced in influence, well into the second half of the twentieth century.

In other countries the eugenic philosophy was taken up more vigorously. In the USA a group of eugenic enthusiasts set up a 'colony' in 1869, and an experimental breeding programme was initiated (McGee, 1891). In many states of the Union, eugenic policies that involved sterilization of the 'morally feeble' and of 'imbeciles' were incorporated into law in the 1920s and 1930s[4] (Paul, 1998). There was in addition often a strong racial element, with particular 'races' being regarded as inferior to others. Even though the equality of all races is now enshrined in US law, racial attitudes die hard; it took many years before there was racial integration in certain southern states. It seems almost too obvious to state that these attitudes and policies are very far from Christian; yet, sadly, the Bible was often quoted in their support.

Eugenic policies were also adopted in Canada and in several European countries, most notably in Nazi Germany, where sterilization (probably involving at least 400,000 people), experiments on humans, compulsory euthanasia and some enforced breeding experiments were all part of the programme (Paul, 1998), in addition to the extermination of millions of Jewish people in the name of racial purity. Little wonder, then, that in modern Germany there is genuine and widespread concern about the applications of modern genetic research. However, other countries also introduced compulsory sterilization on eugenic grounds: eugenic sterilizations continued in

---

3. But note that over 2,000 years ago Plato speculated that society might be improved by selective breeding.

4. It is estimated that at least 30,000 people were sterilized for eugenic reasons in the USA during the 1920s and 1930s; some sterilizations took place after the Second World War, but the practice had ceased by the 1950s.

Canada and Switzerland until the 1960s, and in Sweden until the 1970s (Nuffield Council on Bioethics, 2002b).

The question thus arises: how shall we use our increasing knowledge and understanding of human genetics? It has been thrown into sharp focus by the Human Genome Project, which we now discuss in more detail.

Human genetics and the Human Genome Project

As we described in Chapter 5, long before there was any knowledge about genes there had been an understandable human interest in human inheritance, some of that interest being directed at the inheritance of disease. This focus continued with the formal establishment of genetics as a science; since the middle of the twentieth century one of the main motivations in the study of human genetics has been to understand the genetic basis of disease. There are about 4,500 diseases caused by mutations in single genes; most of them are rare (Strachan and Read, 1996). More common ones include sickle-cell anaemia, cystic fibrosis, achondroplasia (skeletal dwarfism) and X-linked haemophilia. We also now know that genetic mutations are involved in determining predisposition to certain diseases. The known number of these is likely to rise as our knowledge of human genetics increases.

Study of genetic diseases in humans is limited by our inability to undertake mating experiments. For the most part, prior to the advent of DNA analysis, study of the inheritance of human genetic disease depended on who had chosen to have children with whom. If a couple were concerned about the possibility of having a child with a genetic disease, the assessment of genetic risk depended on the pattern of inheritance of the condition in their families and knowledge of the frequency of the particular mutation within the population. Essentially, the couple could be given only a statistical probability, often not very accurate or specific, of a child being born with a particular disease. There were just a few conditions where the estimates of genetic risk could be backed up by biochemical analysis of a blood sample from the child after birth: for instance, in phenylketonuria (see Glossary). Where the diagnosis can be confirmed early in this way, some forms of treatment and/or management of the condition are possible.

The development of recombinant DNA technology in the 1970s was therefore very important. The 'growth' of genes (molecular cloning)[5] in microbial cells, combined with a developing ability to characterize particular DNA sequences, meant that it became possible to investigate directly some of the genetic changes that lead to the development of a disease. The genes involved in several heritable diseases, including cystic fibrosis, had been identified, cloned and characterized by the end of the 1980s, prior to the establishment of the Human Genome Project (see Turnpenny and Bryant, 2002). This in turn meant that diagnostic and detection techniques based on actual gene sequences were becoming available.

In 1988 a consortium of scientists in the USA persuaded Congress that the time was right for the establishment of a coordinated programme to sequence the entire human genome (Shapiro, 1991). The programme was set to run from 1990 to 2005 and, in the USA, $3,000 million was initially allocated to the project. This sum included 5% allocated to study the ethical and social implications of the project.[6] The decision to set up the HGP was not without its critics: in the USA some members of the public (and presumably some members of Congress) believed that the money could have been spent in other ways, raising questions about allocation of limited resources. Even among the science community there were some who, at least at that time, believed the establishment of the project to be a major mistake (Rechsteiner, 1991). Among social commentators too there was some cynicism, with suggestions that in its conception it was 'very American' – appealing to the American psyche by virtue of its scale.

The USA, however, did not go it alone, since the project incorporated human gene analysis already in progress outside the country. About two-thirds of the work has been done in the USA, most of the rest being split between the UK, Germany, France, Japan and Canada. Progress was extremely rapid and indeed exceeded all expectations: by mid-2000, some four and a half years before the formal closure of the project, the sequences of the majority of human genes were known, as were the identities of many disease-causing mutations. One interesting and still-puzzling feature to emerge is that humans and other mammals have only about 30,000 genes (Butler

---

5. Using cultures of microbial cells to make many copies of particular fragments of DNA.

6. <www.ornl.gov/sci/techresources/Human_Genome/elsi/elsi.shtml>.

and Smaglik, 2000), whereas it had been predicted from studies of genetics that we would have about 80,000. One possible explanation for this is that many genes may have multiple functions (and indeed, some multifunctional genes are already known). This in turn implies the existence of complex control mechanisms that regulate multiple gene functions. It also implies that genetic modification of mammals may not be as straightforward as had been previously suggested, notwithstanding the routine production of genetically modified mice for use in biomedical research (see also 'Animal GM: routine or routinely risky?' in Chapter 7).

The recent completion of the mouse genome sequence (see Whitfield, 2002b) enables a fascinating direct comparison between two mammals. Of the mouse's approximately 30,000 genes, all but about 300 have direct equivalents in humans; of the genes that humans possess, several hundred are not found in the mouse. We can see instantly that a very large proportion of human genes and of mouse genes are likely to be involved in the biological functions of being a mammal. As we have noted before, genetics gives us a good picture of our biological nature. Further, in practical terms it means that, for many genes, the mouse is indeed a good model for the study of gene function that is relevant to humans.

Genetics, commerce and ethics

Well before the first draft of the human genome sequence was published there were ethical arguments about using the information. The HGP itself is based in an international network of laboratories that are funded by government agencies and/or charities. They are committed to making the results widely available, the primary sequence data being readily accessible to the whole scientific community. Human genes, however, have a significant commercial relevance as we understand more about genetic disease and predisposition to disease. Possibilities are raised of development of new treatments and of profits for pharmaceutical and biotechnology companies. Thus it was not surprising that a commercial company, Celera Genomics, also undertook to sequence the human genome and, by virtue of major financial investment, managed to 'challenge' the HGP, despite the company's later start. The tensions between the two groups were obvious enough to be noticed by several science journalists commenting on the publication of the first draft (e.g. Marshall, 2000; Smaglik, 2000b). The company would wish to protect its intellectual property, perhaps by patenting the gene sequences, while the HGP itself was committed to contributing to publicly available knowledge. Extensive negotiations led to an uneasy truce and the first draft sequence was indeed published.[7] However, tensions about the use of genetic information remain, and patenting of genes is still one of the contested areas. We discuss this below (see 'Gene patents and medical genetics', below, p. 128).

Human genetics and medicine

Introduction

As predicted, the HGP has provided new evidence about the involvement of genes in human disease; this body of evidence is set to grow as we build on the basic sequence information. The question then is whether the information can truly be used in the relief of human suffering. We discuss this question under a number of headings:

- The challenge
- Genetic diagnosis and screening
- Genetic discrimination
- Gene patents and medical genetics
- The burden of genetic knowledge

The challenge

The current Director of the Human Genome Project is Dr Francis Collins, an evangelical Christian. He, like the present authors, is thrilled with the progress in human genetics and its potential for alleviating suffering. However, the task of applying the knowledge is not straightforward; as a challenge to society, Collins (1999a) has produced a set of questions, including the following:

- Will we successfully shepherd new genetic tests from research into clinical practice? This question includes topics that range from equality of access to resources to support and counselling

---

7. The 'final' version was published in spring 2003: <www.ornl.gov/hgmis>.

for those who have to carry 'genetic knowledge' about themselves or loved ones.

- Will we solve the problem of genetic discrimination?
- Will we arrive at a consensus about the limits of genetic technology for the enhancement of 'desirable' characters? (We discuss this in Chapter 7.)

With these questions in mind, we turn to consider the use of genetic knowledge in medicine.

Genetic diagnosis and screening
These developments have led, over a very short period of time, to the development of diagnostic and screening tests for genetic diseases. This is done by analysing particular genes of individual humans and identifying genetic changes. Such testing can now be done at three different stages of development:

- Postnatal – after birth, in a baby, child or adult
- Prenatal – before birth, but after the embryo has implanted into the wall of the uterus
- Pre-implantation – before the embryo has implanted into the wall of the uterus

Postnatal diagnosis
The direct diagnosis of a limited number of genetic diseases has been available for over twenty years, but the strong focus on human genetics since 1990 has seen the addition to the list of many more. However, the implications of such testing are not always straight-forward. The effects of the gene changes which have been identified may not become clear for a long time, even well into adult life. Many genes have several different functions, so the effects of gene change may be difficult to predict. The extent to which the effects of a gene are expressed also varies from person to person. For some diseases, therefore, the prognosis will be uncertain. In many other conditions the results of testing may bring huge disappointment, as there may be little or no treatment for the particular disease which has been diagnosed. Thus advice about testing should always be realistic, measured and compassionate.

Nevertheless, there are some positive sides to postnatal genetic testing. Where treatment is available, it can be started early in the course of the disease. Even if there is no treatment, knowing that a child has a particular disease starts the process for the family of finding the appropriate support, in education and through social benefit and support groups. It also assists parents to help their children to understand what has gone wrong. It enables the future to be faced and informed decisions to be made about the child's reproductive life in adulthood. Finally, of course, it is a huge relief when testing shows that a child does not have the disease that was thought to be possible.

The screening of children in this way raises the issue of consent. In English law, parents may make decisions about diagnostic testing and treatment for their children who are minors, as it is accepted that small children, particularly, lack competence to give informed consent. Where a disease is present in childhood or will develop in later life and the prognosis is poor, a very considerable burden is placed on the child and the family. A great amount of pastoral care and support may be needed over a long period of time. Christians, at least, may also find strength in the knowledge that God brings good things out of suffering and that he has all the resources needed to face the future. As the psalmist put it:

> My flesh and my heart may fail,
>   but God is the strength of my heart
>   and my portion for ever.
> (Ps. 73:26)

Prenatal diagnosis
Diagnostic tests for some genetic diseases have been carried out during the early stages of pregnancy for more than twenty years (more than thirty years for some chromosomal abnormalities, such as Down syndrome). This was originally done at about the sixteenth week of pregnancy by examining foetal cells from the amniotic fluid which surrounds the baby in the uterus. Nowadays a technique known as chorionic villus sampling is used, in which cells from the edge of the placenta are examined. This can be done as early as the eleventh or twelfth week of a pregnancy. If the test is positive, termination of the pregnancy can be offered. Many people feel more comfortable about a termination at this early stage, rather than four months into the pregnancy. However, whether termination is carried out at twelve weeks or at seventeen weeks, there is no difference in the

ethical arguments surrounding the decision. The life of a potential human being is still being destroyed.

At the time of writing, tests are available for about sixty genetic diseases. Many of these diseases are rare and therefore are not routinely tested for; instead, tests are carried out where the family history indicates that the foetus may be at risk of having a particular genetic disease. Both parents may be carriers of the disease, or they may already have an affected child. The fact that the parents are carriers may not be known until a child is born, as often happens, for example, with cystic fibrosis. Parents then face the choice of whether to allow a prenatal diagnosis to be made. If the foetus is found to have the disease, should the pregnancy be terminated? This raises the whole question of our attitudes towards children who are sick or disabled from birth, as discussed in Chapter 3, where we dealt with the biblical view of humankind as made in the image of God. However, specific issues arise here.

It tends to be the case that the more severe the genetic disease diagnosed before birth, the easier is the decision to terminate the pregnancy, on the grounds that severe suffering is thereby prevented. These views have been further reinforced by influential individuals, undoubtedly motivated by a desire to reduce human suffering but who nevertheless have increased the pressure on parents in relation to decisions about termination of pregnancy. As cited by Peterson (2001: 222), Shaw, a lawyer from the USA, states that it should be a criminal offence to give birth to a child with (the gene mutation that causes) Huntington's disease, while Edwards, one of the two UK pioneers of *in vitro* fertilization, casts his net even wider: 'it will be the sin of the parents to have a child who carries the heavy burden of genetic disease'. This reflects a concern that we have expressed previously (Turnpenny and Bryant, 2002; Bryant and Turnpenny, 2003): that in respect of genetic conditions some members of the medical community have adopted a 'search and destroy' policy.

While the desire to prevent severe suffering may be considered to be admirable, some see it as the beginning of a slide down the slippery slope. What level of suffering and disability should be prevented in this way? How narrow is our concept of normality? Is not this discriminating against disabled people (Shakespeare, 1998; Kuhse, 1999; Messer, 2003)?

In our view, making a right judgment about a foetus who will be born to a life of severe disability and suffering and possible early death is very difficult, because different ethical principles, each laudable in itself, come into conflict. Such children are made in the image of God and loved by him. We have a duty of human love and care towards them. Caring for such a child may draw from the carers remarkable qualities of unselfishness and devotion. Equally, such caring may place enormous, even unbearable, stresses on parents and on their marriage. At times it may be difficult to avoid the conclusion that it would have been better had the child never been born.

Financial factors too may influence decisions. The costs of care to both the family and healthcare providers may be very large indeed. When financial resources are finite, is it just to spend a large sum of money on one such child, thereby diverting resources away from other individuals where treatment would restore them to a good quality of life and economic usefulness? Thus, although the Cyprus government, in setting up a testing programme for thalassaemia accompanied by ready availability of termination for affected foetuses, may well have acted in part out of a desire to reduce human suffering,[8] it is highly likely that financial factors contributed to the decision. Insurance companies, too, especially in those countries where they bear the major costs of healthcare, will be interested in the costs of caring for a child with a genetic disorder. Indeed, there have been cases reported in the USA of healthcare insurance being refused for children brought into the world after a positive prenatal diagnosis of a genetic condition (see Peterson, 2001). The insurance companies would presumably have exerted pressure on the prospective parents to terminate the pregnancy; in withholding cover they are discriminating not only against the child on account of its genetic condition but against the parents on account of their principles.

There are other approaches to dealing with severe genetic illness: for instance, some religious communities have developed methods other than termination of pregnancy for reducing the incidence of such diseases. Rabbi Joseph Ekstein of New York set up a system for testing all young people for carrier status in respect of Tay-Sachs disease. The results are recorded, but in a coded system; they are not revealed to the young people who are tested. However, if two young people begin to think of marrying each other, they can find out, from the authorities keeping the records, whether they carry the Tay-Sachs

---

8. Most thalassaemias are painful and crippling conditions, usually leading to death before the age of twenty.

mutation. If they are both carriers, they are advised not to marry. Some Christian communities have adopted a similar approach: in Cyprus, for example, where, since 1978, the state has funded free testing for carrier status in respect of thalassaemia, the Orthodox Church since 1981 has insisted that all couples planning a church wedding should be tested. Where both parties are carriers, that couple is strongly advised not to marry. Both these communities thus avoid tough decisions about termination of pregnancy. This will of course be hard on two young people who are in love; this emphasizes once more, in both Jewish and Christian settings, the biblical sense of community in supporting one another.

Lastly, in making the decision to terminate a pregnancy there is another important family consideration. Suppose the parents already have an affected child: say, with cystic fibrosis. They then discover that the child they are expecting has the same disease and decide to have a termination. What does that say about the child they have already? Is their love for the first child diminished because they do not want to have another similar child? Would they have preferred not to have the first child, had they known that he or she would suffer from cystic fibrosis? They may, of course, argue that by terminating the pregnancy they are preventing the child's future suffering; but what does that say about the suffering of the child they already have, who must endure it?

Termination of pregnancy or induced abortion, for whatever reason it is carried out, is inevitably a recurring topic of moral and ethical debate. In the UK, under the terms of the Abortion Act 1967, criteria for offering termination included the likelihood of the baby suffering 'congenital disorders'. The latter term covers genetic and chromosomal disorders and other developmental lesions: for example, termination of pregnancy is offered if the chromosomal disorder Down syndrome is detected. Christians are divided in their views on abortion. Those who take the most conservative position, including most Roman Catholics and many evangelicals, are opposed to abortion under any circumstances unless there is a very high risk to the life of the mother. They hold that the commandment to refrain from killing (Exod. 20:13; Deut. 5:17) extends to the unborn. They suggest that the biblical imperative to care for the weak and those in need of protection must be applied to the unborn (see e.g. P. Taylor, 2002). These views are supported by quotation of the small number of biblical texts that refer to pregnancy (such as Ps. 139). Parents who hold this view will bring to term foetuses that are known to suffer from severe congenital conditions and will usually refuse prenatal tests on the grounds that they could not be persuaded to terminate a pregnancy. However, many Christians are not totally opposed to abortion (see discussion in Wyatt, 1998), allowing it on grounds that include severe congenital (including genetic) abnormalities. A very detailed analysis from an evangelical perspective has been presented by the US theologian and ethicist Richard Hays (Hays, 1996). He maintains that biblical imperatives to refrain from murder were applicable only to existing humans. He further suggests that the biblical passages that mention pregnancy do not assist in ascribing a moral status to the foetus. Indeed, he is quite critical of those who would cite proof texts to support their case, because 'the Bible contains no texts about abortion' (Hays, 1996: 446).[9] Hays therefore suggests that, as we have seen before in this volume, we need to apply general biblical principles rather than look for very specific guidance. He reaches the conclusion that abortion is contrary to the general ethical tenor of Scripture and, in particular, that it runs counter to the view that all human life is a gift from God. While that view leads him to oppose abortion, he does make specific exceptions for pregnancies that occur as a result of rape or incest and for situations where the life of the mother is in genuine danger. In relation to the life of the mother, most Christians outside the Roman Catholic Church place a higher value on someone who is established as a fully self-conscious human – one who is, in the language of moral philosophy, 'the subject of a life' – than they do on an unborn child that has not yet realized its potential to become a fully self-conscious human. Concerning rape and incest, Hays's own words are helpful (Hays, 1996: 456):

> The argument to justify abortion rests heavily upon experiential warranty: we recoil instinctively from requiring a woman to bear the burden of a child conceived through an act of violence against her ... such an appeal to experience carries considerably more weight in theological argument in a case – such as this one – where there are no direct New Testament teachings on the subject. My own view would be that such exceptions are certainly justifiable options for Christians.

---

9. Exodus 21:22–25 refers to accidentally caused miscarriage.

On the matter of handicap Hays is much less clear and indeed makes no specific reference to severe genetic abnormalities. He thus evades the very difficult decisions faced by parents who are told that the baby has a congenital condition that will result in severe handicap and a very short and possibly pain-ridden life. He does, however, suggest that the church has a duty to support those parents who choose not to terminate a pregnancy on the grounds of handicap, thus sharing our view that the church should be a community that tries, with the help of the Holy Spirit, to live out the values of the kingdom. This reflects the statement of Jesus that we are 'light' and 'salt' (Matt. 5:13–16); although the passage is applied, in our very individualistic Western culture, primarily to individual Christians, in the time of Jesus it would have been applied equally strongly to the community of believers.

Hays concedes that different Christians, who share an equal respect for the Scriptures, may well come to different conclusions in specific cases (as we noted in Chapter 2). In general, however, when it comes to deciding about abortion in relation to congenital disease, handicap or abnormality, those who do not totally oppose abortion will base their judgment on factors such as the likely severity of the condition in question. As we have indicated in Chapter 3, all humans, whether able-bodied or disabled, are created in the image of God. We equally recognize, however, that some genetic conditions are so severe, in respect of the likely suffering and poor quality of life of the infant, that some prospective parents will opt for an abortion. The problem, of course, is in deciding where the line should be drawn.

As the range of prenatal tests and diagnoses has widened, so decision-making for prospective parents has become more difficult. The availability of a wider range of tests may appear to increase parental choice, but in fact may intensify the ethical dilemmas. Concern has been expressed, not only by opponents of abortion but also by various disability support groups, that pressure may be put on prospective parents to terminate a pregnancy even when the genetic condition detected is manageable within a fulfilled and fruitful life.

Pre-implantation genetic diagnosis
A more recent approach to this problem is to make the diagnosis of genetic disease before the early embryo is implanted into the wall of the uterus. This avoids having to decide whether or not to have the pregnancy terminated. Where a couple is at known risk of having a

child with a genetic disease they may opt to become pregnant by *in vitro* fertilization. Several embryos are produced. They are tested in the laboratory at the eight-cell stage for the genetic disease. Embryos free from the disease are then implanted into the mother's uterus. Those with the disease are discarded.

Whether or not this procedure is ethical will depend on the view taken about the status of the early human embryo. If one takes the view that human life begins at implantation, this is an acceptable way of preventing genetic disease from developing. If one believes that human life begins at fertilization (see discussion in Chapter 3), it is no more justifiable to discard diseased embryos than it is to abort an affected foetus.

When deciding whether or not to opt for pre-implantation genetic diagnosis (PGD), a couple must also consider two other factors. First, in the UK *in vitro* fertilization is funded by only a handful of National Health Service providers (although this is about to change), so the considerable cost of the procedure may have to be met by the couple themselves. Secondly, it requires a major commitment from the couple. The production of eggs has to be stimulated by drugs. The eggs are harvested and the embryos are implanted by surgical procedures. The demands on time and the emotional strain may therefore be considerable.

New ethical dilemmas in this area continue to arise. Should these techniques be used not only to avoid giving birth to a child with a genetic disease but also to treat a child who already has a genetic disease? The scenario is that a couple have a child with a genetic disease that may be treated by stem cells from a suitable donor. They then undergo *in vitro* fertilization and pre-implantation diagnosis of the embryos so produced. A disease-free embryo is implanted into the mother's uterus and a normal child is born. Stem cells from this child are then used to treat the first child. The first such case, which we have discussed more fully elsewhere (Turnpenny and Bryant, 2002; Bryant and Turnpenny, 2003), occurred in the USA and involved selecting against Fanconi anaemia (FA) but also for a tissue match to a sister suffering from FA. In the UK the HFEA guidelines were altered early in 2002 to consider, on a case-by-case basis, requests for PGD with tissue typing; permission has been granted in one such case. The ethical concern here is that to create an embryo in order to be a stem-cell donor uses the new child as a commodity, albeit with the very worthy motive of saving the life of an existing child. However, the HFEA has argued that, since the new child benefits by being free of the genetic disease, he or she is not merely a commodity. A further development is to use this method for the treatment of a child who has a non-genetic disease such as leukaemia, which is a form of cancer of the white blood cells. At present the treatment of such a child includes finding a sibling or other family member whose tissues match those of the child, taking bone marrow from the sibling under a general anaesthetic and then transfusing these bone-marrow cells into the child with leukaemia. The donated bone-marrow cells then 'take' and produce normal white blood cells. However, by the technique of *in vitro* fertilization and embryo selection it is possible to produce a sibling baby with a perfect tissue match to that of the leukaemic child. Umbilical-cord stem cells or, if necessary, bone-marrow from this sibling can then be used successfully to treat the sick child. It is difficult to avoid the conclusion that such a sibling *is* being brought into the world primarily for the benefit of another person and is therefore being used as a commodity, however much that sibling may be loved in his or her own right. The HFEA originally ruled that since such a procedure is of no direct benefit to the sibling (there is no selection against a genetic disease) it may not be performed in the UK. This ruling, however, is likely to be reversed.

Our readers will thus appreciate the exquisite difficulties in making ethical decisions in this area, emphasizing the need for wisdom. However, in the UK in 2002 and 2003, the situation became even more complex. First, the House of Commons Science and Technology Committee published a report[10] criticizing, *inter alia*, the change in the HFEA guidelines. The report stated that the decision went beyond the Authority's public consultation on PGD and should therefore have been subject to debate in Parliament rather than being taken by the HFEA itself, although there is actually no evidence of a widespread public rejection of the HFEA's decision. But some members of the public, including those in 'pro-life' organizations, have expressed their concern that PGD in general, and selection of donor embryos in particular, lead to the discarding of the rejected embryos.[11] One such organization, Comment on Reproductive

---

10. Available on the House of Commons website.
11. We discussed views on the ethical status of the pre-implantation embryo in Chapter 3.

Ethics (CORE), obtained early in 2003 a High Court decision to ban the use of PGD to select embryos as stem-cell donors. Their case was based, at one level, on opposition to the creation of embryos as commodities and on concern about 'designer babies'. The details of CORE's submission clearly indicated, however, that the real reason for bringing the case was their view that the pre-implantation embryo is a human person, with all that that implies. The HFEA appealed against this decision and in April 2003 the Court of Appeal overturned the earlier High Court ban. This case provides a clear demonstration of the complex relationship between personal ethics and public policy and the difficulties of deciding the extent to which personal ethics should shape policy. Furthermore, it illustrates the clash between the deontological position (the early embryo must be protected under all circumstances) and the consequentialist position (discarding unsuitable embryos will save the life of a child). We also note the irony of the fact that 'pro-life' organizations are arguing against a procedure that would save the life of a child. Thus Paul Tulley, the General Secretary of the Society for Protection of the Unborn Child, is quoted as saying, 'Just because a child's life is at stake does not mean that you discard all ethics.' However, what has in fact happened is that, in a situation where a decision actually had to be made, one ethical position has been ruled as being more appropriate than another in making that decision. Some have suggested that this simply represents situation ethics dressed up as compassion, but that does not do justice to the complexity of the circumstances and the care taken in reaching a decision. There will always be disagreement when two different ethical principles are brought to bear against each other, and doubtless different readers of this text will reach different conclusions.

Genetic discrimination

We now move from discussion of the implications of genetic diagnosis in medicine to consider wider social and ethical implications. The number of genetic tests routinely available will increase rapidly as scientists apply the basic genomic data to the understanding of human disease. As we have indicated, these tests may be applied to adults, to children, to foetuses and to pre-implantation embryos created by IVF. Currently, most of the available tests are for mutations which are absolutely or strongly predictive of the occurrence of genetic disease, albeit that some of these genetic diseases are late-onset conditions such as Huntington's disease. The availability of these tests raises the possibility of discrimination on genetic grounds in matters of life assurance, health insurance (in countries where there is no state provision of health care) and employment. Indeed, there is evidence, especially from the USA, that such discrimination is already occurring: for example, we noted earlier that health insurance had been refused for a child born with a genetic disease, because the insurance company believed that the pregnancy should have been terminated after a diagnostic genetic test. The whole issue is undoubtedly complex. Life-assurance companies may argue, for example, that it is perfectly 'fair' to deny life-assurance cover to (or greatly to increase the premiums of) people carrying a gene that is strongly predictive of a serious disease in later life. It is not right, they will add, that the financial burden of insuring the lives of such people should be borne partly by those who are free of such conditions. It could equally well be pointed out, however, that until the genetic test became available the financial burden had indeed been spread among all the company's clients, so why should this not continue? Indeed, the whole basis of insurance is that the many support the few. For instance, in any one year most policy-holders do not make a claim, but the claims of those who do are met by the premiums of the majority of policy-holders. This seems to us to be a clear example of the Christian mandate to share in bearing one another's burdens. Our own position is therefore that insurers should not discriminate on the basis of information from genetic tests.

In employment, too, an employer may argue that certain genetic conditions actually make some people unsuitable for particular jobs, just as some more straightforward physical impairments do.

If the situation is complex now, it will become more so in the future. For example, as Francis Collins states (Collins, 2001), there is a sense in which all illness has a genetic component: different people are differently resistant or vulnerable to bacterial and viral infections, are differently reactive to factors such as environmental carcinogens, and so on. It is likely that tests for some of these quantitative traits will also become available (see also Chapter 9). There is then the possibility that employers will check on the vulnerability of prospective employees, for example, to the common cold or influenza and hence the likelihood of their being frequently absent from work. More worrying still might be positive discrimination in favour of those who are less likely to succumb to the effects of a particular carcinogen that, because of poor safety practices, is present in the workplace.

Readers who wish for a fuller discussion of this complex topic from a Christian perspective are referred to Peterson (2001). Here, we simply reiterate that the Christian church must be a caring community. Those who suffer from genetic disease or who carry the knowledge that they may do so, whether or not they have thereby suffered discrimination, are equally our neighbours. In the Christian community, the body of Christ, there is a sense in which we all suffer if one suffers (1 Cor. 12:26). We should support one another, and that imperative becomes even more demanding in relation to those who are indeed, for any reason, excluded from healthcare or employment (see e.g. Matt. 25:40; Jas. 2:1).

Gene patents and medical genetics

As we mentioned briefly in connection with commercial interests in plant genetics (see Chapter 5) and in human genetics ('Human genetics and medicine', in Chapter 6), one of the controversial topics is gene patenting. There are many factors to consider here, but for us the key question is whether a gene sequence is an invention, which would be patentable, or the discovery of a natural entity, which would not. Biotechnology companies have argued that although genes exist in nature, the making of copies of genes allows them to be classed as inventions. We side here with the European Ecumenical Commission for Church and Society and with the theologians Esther Reed and Audrey Chapman, who believe that this is merely a fudge. Their view (see EECCS, 1996; Chapman, 2002; Reed, 2003) and ours is that genes are natural entities and therefore are not patentable. Their inventor is God; they are the work of his hands; even though the biblical writers knew nothing of genes, they certainly identified God as the author of life and of biological diversity (e.g. Job 39 – 41). Among secular organizations that have considered this topic, the Nuffield Council on Bioethics (2002a) also reached the conclusion that genes should not be patented. Nevertheless, some human gene sequences have been patented and this has had some effect on the availability of certain genetic tests. For example, Williams-Jones (2002) examines in detail the patenting of the BRCA 1 and BRCA 2 genes, mutations of which give a very high lifetime probability of contracting breast and/or ovarian cancer. The patents on these genes are held by a Canadian biotechnology company, Myriad, and the

American pharmaceutical company Eli-Lilley is licensed to exploit the patents (with payment of royalties to Myriad). Williams-Jones concludes that in Canada, in the USA and in Europe, the price of tests for mutations of these genes is higher than it would have been had they not been patented and that this is preventing some healthcare providers from using the tests.

The commercial use of human genetic information is yet another complex issue. Certainly the pharmaceutical and biotechnology companies, with all their background experience of bringing bio-medical discoveries into the marketplace, have a role to play in the application of genetic knowledge to clinical practice. Indeed, as we have already stated in Chapter 5, we are not opposed to the making of profits per se. When the profit motive begins to exclude people from healthcare, however, then surely it must be restrained (see e.g. Jas. 5:1–6).

Such a situation runs counter to statements from the Human Genome Organization (HUGO) that 'the genome is the common heritage of humanity',[12] or from HUGO's chair of ethics that 'in the interests of human solidarity, we owe each other a share in common goods, such as health' (Knoppers, 2000). The challenge presented by Francis Collins (1999a), that we must ensure equality of access, remains with us.

The burden of genetic knowledge

In our informal surveys of our students, there is nearly always a majority who say that they would like to know if they carried a gene that either caused or gave a strong predisposition to genetic disease. However, this is not necessarily true of society in general. For example, testing for Huntington's disease, a serious, late-onset degenerative condition demonstrating 100% penetrance, is requested much less frequently than would be predicted from knowledge of the number of families that are at risk. There may be many reasons for not wishing to know (see Bryant and Turnpenny, 2003), but it is clear that, for some, ignorance is bliss. This topic of the burden of genetic knowledge is dealt with sociologically in several chapters in the excellent book *The Troubled Helix* (Marteau and Richards, 1996) and from a Christian standpoint, although rather less extensively, by

---

12. See <www.gene.ucl.ac.uk/hugo/benefit.html>.

Peterson (2001). It is not our intention here to provide a detailed treatment of this topic, but we have already noted the biblical command to bear one another's burdens. In order to help extend that burden-bearing to genetic knowledge, we now present a series of questions that have arisen in genetic case work. Doubtless different readers would, if they were affected, answer these questions differently. That does not matter; what we are trying to explain here is the type of personal dilemma that arises in respect of some forms of genetic knowledge.

- Because of my family history I know that I am likely to be an unaffected carrier of a gene that causes a serious and so far untreatable condition. Do I request a test for that gene? If the test is positive, do I tell my partner or spouse?
- Knowledge of my family history informs me that I have a fifty–fifty chance of possessing a gene that around the age of forty will cause a serious neuro-degenerative disease for which there is no treatment. Do I want the test? If the test is positive, should I tell my partner, or my children?
- I am currently healthy but know that I have a gene that is very likely to cause serious health problems and possibly death in middle age. Who else should know?

In all these cases so far, we can add three more questions:

- Should the knowledge go outside the family, for example to employers or to insurance companies? Do they have the right to know?
- How do I feel about the knowledge that I will, or am very likely to, suffer from a possibly lethal condition? (The term 'pre-patient' has been used to describe people who are in this position.)
- How do other family members regard such pre-patients?

The remaining questions concern the testing of children who are too young to give informed consent.

- My family history suggests that my child may possess a gene that will cause a serious late-onset condition. Should we have the child tested? If the test is positive, how do we then treat that child? Will the knowledge alter family dynamics? At what age should the child be told? What if, on reaching the age at which an individual can give consent, the child decides that he or she would actually have preferred not to know?

All these questions represent real human dilemmas. Even if we believe that we know what we would do, we must not assume that other people – even those who share our faith – will reach the same answer. The church community needs to support in a non-judgmental manner those who are dealing with such dilemmas: listening and, if asked, providing advice.[13] We suggest that the over-emphasis on individual salvation that is so prevalent in much Western evangelicalism is not helpful here. There is a clear need to re-awaken a sense of Christian community which leads to an environment of compassion and support for those who struggle with these and other issues.

Is the new genetics the new eugenics?

There is concern that extended premarital, prenatal and pre-implantation genetic testing will be perceived as a form of eugenics. The clear motive for doing such testing is to prevent the birth of those who would suffer from a serious genetic condition. As such it clearly meets the definitions of eugenics: 'well-born', 'good birth' and so on. Indeed, the use of human genetic information to inform decisions about childbearing has been called 'eugenics with a smiling face'. The problem will come in defining what is deemed to be serious: we have already noted the tendency to request or to offer terminations of pregnancy for conditions which hitherto had been successfully managed within a fulfilled and happy life. If this trend persists, and we see marginalization of the disabled and a narrowing of our perceptions of normality (see, for example, Shakespeare, 1998; Nuffield Council on Bioethics, 2002b), then eugenics will have lost its smiling face.

But let us refocus. We have already mentioned the Ashkenazi Jewish community of New York, where the carrier frequency for Tay-Sachs is 1 in 25 and where the religious authorities keep a record of the carrier status of every person. The advice to two young people

---

13. This model of community is described beautifully by Hays (1996) in respect of abortion.

who are carriers not to marry, nearly always accepted, has resulted in new cases of Tay-Sachs being virtually eliminated from that community.[14] Within the community the programme is called in Hebrew *Dor Yeshorim*, meaning 'the generation of the righteous'. While we will certainly contest the idea that freedom from Tay-Sachs may be equated with righteousness, many will share an enthusiasm for the outworkings of the programme, achieved without recourse to termination of pregnancy. Eugenics can have a smiling face but, as stated earlier in this chapter ('Genetics and eugenics'), we must remember what can happen when eugenics is used for social engineering.

Do we ascribe too much to genes?

In the subsection 'Human genetics and medicine', we presented some challenges laid down by Francis Collins in respect of the use of human genetic information. However, we have saved one of those challenges until this point in the chapter: namely, how will we counter the tendency to genetic reductionism or determinism – the belief that 'It is all in our genes'?

In Chapter 3 we made it very clear that we do not regard humans as being merely the product of their genes. Indeed, we showed how even those who apparently hold such views actually find them very difficult, if not impossible, to live by. And yet the media still love the idea. Influential magazines and newspapers in the UK and the USA (and doubtless in other countries too) present articles that proclaim the existence of a 'gay gene', a gene that determines marital fidelity (or not, as the case may be), a gene that determines criminality, a gene for a happy disposition and so on. The common feature of all these stories is that they are wrong, and scientists are increasingly willing to state that they are. As clearly demonstrated in the excellent study by the Nuffield Council on Bioethics (2002b) of the relationship between genetics and behaviour, we cannot identify one-to-one correspondences between a gene and 'a behaviour' (and in most cases we cannot specifically define and quantify the behaviour about which

---

14. See the article 'Why genetics is here to stay', by Walter Truett Anderson, posted on the Pacific News website, <www.pacificnews.org/jinn/stories/columns/heresies/950727-eugenics.html>.

we are speaking).[15] As is clearly pointed out in the Nuffield Council's report, there is no 'genetic defence' in respect of antisocial or criminal behaviour.[16] Human beings do indeed have free will and are able to exercise it in making decisions about right and wrong.

What, then, do we make of the statement by James Watson, of 'double helix' fame and first Director of the Human Genome Project, on the occasion of the publication of the first draft of the sequence, that 'we will now know who we really are'? In terms of our position within evolutionary biology, it contains an element of truth. As we noted previously, humans share much of their genetic heritage with other mammals, especially the great apes, but also possess a genetic distinctiveness from them. But who I am, or who you are, cannot be defined in terms of three billion base pairs. John Wyatt, the distinguished Christian doctor and writer, puts it in this way: 'We will never understand what it means to be human by analysis of the human genome' (Wyatt, 2003). How heartily we agree with him.

There is, however, one more area in which we may ascribe too much to genes, and that is their role in disease. Yes, our genetic make-up may specify that we will suffer from a genetic condition, or have a high predisposition to a condition, or be vulnerable to particular viral infections. However, except for those genetic diseases with a 100% penetrance, other factors come into play. These certainly include diet and lifestyle, both of which may be informed by genetic knowledge. But, on a worldwide scale, the major factors determining the occurrence of disease are poverty and poor living conditions. In many less-developed countries life expectancy is, on average, too short for the occurrence of late-onset diseases. Even in highly developed countries we can see the effect of these social factors on health. So, while genes are important, they are not everything. There is a tendency in some sectors of the medical community to believe that genes will have the last word. We have already seen this in

---

15. Even the scientific press is not immune from making these gross over-simplifications. In its edition of 29 March 2003, the *New Scientist* reported: 'Binge-eating gene discovered'. In fact this mutation causes a metabolic disorder – a malfunction in the signalling system that helps to regulate food intake. It has nothing to do with bulimia, an eating disorder in which binge-eating is often followed by deliberately induced vomiting.

16. See also the detailed theological and philosophical analysis by Holmes Rolston (1999).

relation to the termination of pregnancy: the supposed finality of the genetic diagnosis may be considered by some as taking priority over the possibility of managing the condition and over parental wishes to have the child anyway. On the wider medical scene, over-emphasis on genetics may divert our attention from the need to deal with these questions of poverty and living conditions, both in our own country and in the wider world. We are reminded once again of the judgment of the sheep and the goats (Matt. 25:31–46), in which failing to treat others – particularly the disadvantaged and marginalized – with compassion is taken as failure to commit to Jesus.

Overview and summary

In this long chapter we have seen how modern genetic techniques have given us immense power to analyse genes. This has led, among other things, to various genome projects in which the main aim has been to describe the sequence of bases – the building-blocks of DNA – of complete genomes and thence to identify all the genes in particular organisms. These projects have provided, and are still providing, extensive information on the structure, function and malfunction of genes and will provide a resource for genetic research for many years to come. The information provided by genetic research is revealing both the complexity and the beauty of gene control mechanisms; as Christians, we are moved to praise as we see the hand of the Creator in all this. Indeed, we may agree with Copernicus, who regarded research and discovery as worship:

> To know the mighty works of God, to comprehend his wisdom and majesty and power, to appreciate in degree the wonderful workings of his laws, surely must be a pleasing and acceptable mode of worship to the Most High, to whom ignorance cannot be more grateful than knowledge. (Quoted by Collins, 1999a.)

However, with increasing knowledge comes increasing responsibility, especially for the way in which the knowledge is used. This is particularly exemplified by our increasing knowledge of human genetics, arising both from the Human Genome Project and from cognate research programmes. The potential for both benefit and harm is enormous. We have seen that the biomedical community has an increasing ability to detect genetic disease and that in many instances this can lead to at least symptomatic treatment.[17] This is clearly good, but there are also negative aspects. Diagnosis of a condition for which there is no effective treatment or management may impose a great emotional burden on the person carrying the mutation, especially if the condition is late-onset (and therefore not yet apparent). The need for a network of support for such people is clear and we have suggested that the church, the community of followers of Jesus, has a clear mandate in the sharing of such burdens.

Further ethical and social issues are raised when we consider prenatal genetic diagnosis. The assumption in applying genetic tests to foetuses is that, if a serious genetic condition is detected, the prospective parents will seek termination of the pregnancy (abortion). Many Christians are totally opposed to abortion and, if they hold that position, will not wish to undergo prenatal diagnosis, even if family history predicts the possibility of a severe genetic condition. The two authors of this volume are not totally opposed to abortion, although we have very serious reservations about the current 'abortion on demand' climate. In respect of genetic illness, we recognize that there are conditions which cause much suffering in the context of a very short infant life, and that in these cases most non-Christians and many Christians will agree that the pregnancy should be terminated. We emphasize again the need for the church to provide care and support for couples in these situations. However, the real problem with the ever-increasing range of genetic tests available for prenatal application is that abortions may now be offered for conditions or disabilities that had previously been managed in childhood and adulthood. Obviously, the decision will lie with the parents, acting on the advice of the clinician, but in our view this development is disturbing. It can lead to a narrowing of our view of normality, and some have perceived it as covert discrimination against the disabled.

The issue of abortion is avoided if a couple at risk of producing a child with a genetic condition opt for *in vitro* fertilization followed by pre-implantation diagnosis. They thus ensure that only embryos that do not possess the faulty gene(s) are inserted into the woman's womb. Of course, for those who hold that the very earliest embryo is a human person the discarding of embryos is as unacceptable as abortion. But

---

17. For a discussion of direct treatment of the faulty genes themselves, see Chapter 8.

readers who share our view of the ethical status of the early embryo (Chapter 3) will find this type of diagnosis acceptable, albeit recognizing that *in vitro* fertilization is not without its problems. Ethical difficulties clearly arise, however, when pre-implantation diagnosis is used to select embryos which, on being born as babies, may act as stem-cell donors for older siblings who suffer from a genetic or (more controversially) from a non-genetic condition. The relief of suffering in the older sibling is a very positive consequence of this procedure and on balance we have no specific moral objections to it. Nevertheless, the danger of regarding the embryo, and hence the baby who will be born, as a commodity is all too apparent. The debate about this application of pre-implantation diagnosis will doubtless continue; the Christian community and society in general need a great deal of wisdom in making decisions on this issue.

Another pressing issue that arises from our increasing genetic knowledge is the possibility of discrimination against individuals on genetic grounds. This may occur in relation to health insurance and life assurance and to employment. Those in these areas who may wish to discriminate against people with particular genetic conditions may well justify that discrimination within their own ethical frameworks. Further, it will be obvious that some conditions and disabilities, whether or not genetically caused, make it very difficult to undertake certain types of work. Nevertheless, we must be constantly on our guard against the possibility of marginalizing the disabled: it is part of our Christian mandate to ensure that everyone has the opportunity to play as full a part as possible in society (and, it is to be hoped, in the church).

Finally, we need to remind ourselves that genes are not everything. It is very important that we do not fall into the trap of believing that 'genes are us', whether in relation to health and disease or to life in general. Over-emphasis on genes can lead to ignoring social and lifestyle factors in health and disease. It can result in denying the validity of emotional experience, free will and altruistic behaviour. It can cause us to ascribe social problems such as homelessness to genes (and therefore foster the idea that there is nothing we can do for the socially marginalized, since they are genetically determined to be that way). Most important of all, it denies our spiritual dimension: that we are made in the image of God and are fully human in relationship with him. As Jesus put it, 'I have come that they may have life, and have it to the full' (John 10:10b).

7. ENHANCEMENT AND THERAPY: GENETIC MODIFICATION OF ANIMALS AND HUMANS

You made him a little lower than the heavenly beings
  and crowned him with glory and honour.
You made him ruler over the works of your hands...
(Ps. 8:5–6a)

Man is neither angel nor beast and it is unfortunately the case that anyone trying to act the angel acts the beast ... It is dangerous to explain too clearly to man how like he is to the animals without pointing out his greatness. It is also dangerous to make too much of his greatness without his vileness. It is still more dangerous to leave him in ignorance of both. Man must not be allowed to believe that he is either equal to animals or to angels, nor to be unaware of either, but he must know both.
(Blaise Pascal, Pensée 358)

Introduction

Initial success in the genetic modification of animal cells was achieved as long ago as the late 1970s, and techniques for the genetic modification of non-human mammals (as opposed to just cells) were first developed in the early 1980s. This field has been recently reviewed (Turnpenny and Bryant, 2002; Bryant and Turnpenny, 2003) and this brief account is based on references cited by those reviewers.

There are two basic procedures by which this genetic modification in non-human mammals can be achieved. The more widely used procedure is the introduction of the foreign DNA into an unfertilized egg cell (oocyte) prior to *in vitro* fertilization or into the newly fertilized egg. The embryo, which now carries 'foreign' (exogenous) genes, is then introduced into the uterus of a suitable potential mother in the 'normal' fashion. If a pregnancy is established successfully (this is a big 'if' – see below), a *transgenic* (genetically modified) mammal will eventually be born; furthermore, it will pass on the new gene to subsequent generations.

It was quickly established that not only could foreign genes be introduced in this way but it was possible to control the timing and/or location of the genes' activity (i.e. their pattern of expression) if the foreign DNA also contained the relevant gene-promoter sequence, that is the gene's on/off switch. The early experiments were done with mice; it soon became apparent that the success rate for birth of baby mice from embryos that had been genetically manipulated was only about 25% of that achieved with non-manipulated embryos. Indeed, as these studies were extended to other mammals low success rates were seen to be a general problem. Although this figure has been improved on since then, it is still clear that the success rate is lower with transgenic embryos than with non-GM embryos. Thus the overall live birth rate for transgenic farm animals such as sheep and cattle may be as low as 2–4%.

The second main approach to genetic modification of mammals is to insert the foreign DNA into stem cells[1] that have been removed from a pre-implantation embryo (obtained either by *in vitro* fertilization or by removal from the female mammal). The modified cells are replaced in the embryo, which is then inserted into the uterus and brought to term. The foreign gene is passed on to the next generation via the germline (that is, by those cells that give rise to the gametes or 'germ cells', the eggs and sperm). Although not generally applicable to larger animals such as sheep or cattle (or humans!), it is a useful alternative procedure for animals with a short generation time, such as mice.

Animal GM – routine or routinely risky?

In the later sections of this chapter we discuss the possible application of these techniques to humans. Before doing so, however, we need to raise some technical problems. Leaving theological and general ethical considerations aside for the moment, these problems should certainly affect our thinking, at least in a pragmatic or even consequentialist way. First, animal chromosomes (like plant chromosomes: see

---

1. Cells with the potential to give rise to all the different cell types within the body: see Chapter 8.

Chapter 5) are complex structures and very little is known about the factors that determine where in the chromosomes the foreign gene is inserted. Thus, in genetically modified animals, the *level* of expression of the exogenous gene (i.e. how active the gene is) varies considerably from animal to animal. This variation is mainly put down to *position effects* (variations caused by incorporation of the exogenous gene at different places within the recipient genome, as discussed in relation to plants in Chapter 5). It would obviously be preferable if position-effect variability could be eliminated; significant effort has therefore been expended in trying to target foreign genes to specific places in the chromosomes. There has been some limited success with mice (Thompson et al., 1989) and more recently in sheep (McCreath, et al., 2000), but it is certainly not yet routine. This means that the level of expression of the foreign gene must be monitored in as many GM animals as possible (which for larger animals may not be very many) in order to select the best. Secondly, although the inserted genes are inherited from generation to generation, the extent to which those genes are expressed in subsequent generations may vary.[2]

We need to be aware of such problems in any discussion of the application of GM techniques in humans (see 'Genetic modification of humans', 'Germline therapy' and 'Genetic enhancement' below). Nevertheless, these operational difficulties have not prevented the use of GM animals in medical and biomedical research and in bio-technology. For example, mice can be modified with mutant genes which cause diseases including cystic fibrosis and Huntington's disease, or with oncogenes (genes that when activated cause the animal to develop cancer). In the UK alone, many hundreds of thousands of such GM mice are used each year in biomedical research. There is also current research on modifying pigs so that their organs may be used in human transplants, and it is well established that farm animals such as sheep can be genetically modified to produce pharmaceutical proteins in their milk. Indeed, one of the reasons for cloning the sheep that provided the genetic material for Dolly was a wish to be able to replicate genetically a sheep in which an economically important gene was especially active (Griffin, 2002).

---

2. There are good biological explanations for this variability in the progeny. The technical details lie outside the scope of this chapter, but interested readers are referred to Bryant and Turnpenny, 2003.

GM and animal welfare

The development and increasing use of genetic manipulation of animals has led to further discussion of animal welfare and of human use of and attitudes towards non-human animals. These topics were mentioned briefly in Chapters 4 and 5, but are brought into sharper focus by genetic manipulation and cloning. There can be no doubt that genetically modifying animals for biotechnology or for research on animal or human genes is an instrumental use of animals. Furthermore, many of the animals used as 'models' in the study of human genetic disease suffer physical and physiological malfunction and, in some cases, actual pain as a result of carrying the mutant gene. The question then is whether we are justified in creating (for instance) sheep that produce pharmaceuticals in their milk, pigs with 'human-friendly' organs, or mice that develop tumours.

As we discussed in Chapter 4, we cannot interpret the term *dominion* to mean unbridled freedom to do what we like with the natural world. In our usage, the term *stewardship* better conveys an appropriate attitude to nature. But what does this mean in relation to animals? Throughout both the Old and New Testaments, human-kind used animals in various ways, including religious sacrifices, food (both direct, i.e. meat, and indirect, e.g. milk), various forms of labour (including transport) and provision of material for clothing. All these are instrumental uses of animals but nowhere in the Bible is there any indication that such uses are wrong. Old Testament law, however, also embodied a respect for domestic animals and a requirement to consider their welfare. Working animals were to enjoy a sabbath rest (Exod. 20:8–10; Deut. 5:12–14) and were not to be prevented from 'snacking' while they were working (Deut. 25:4). Respect for animals is also implied in Jesus' parable of the lost sheep (Matt. 18:12–14; Luke 15:3–7). Clearly the point of the parable is God's love and concern for the lost sinner, for whom he searches and whom he brings back to the sheepfold of his kingdom. But the picture is based on a shepherd's concern for the welfare of the animal, not simply for economic reasons but for its own sake. Our factory-farming techniques, especially with poultry, are a long way from this attitude of welfare towards the animals we are using. For example, factory-farmed poultry have been intensively selectively bred for weight. As a result they suffer from chronic skeletal disorders.

They are clearly unable to perform many actions normal for their species, and indeed are physically prevented from doing so by the confined space in which they are kept and in some instances by major trimming of their beaks. They also exhibit many of the symptoms of stress. Does not all this suggest that we should return to a more compassionate approach in the treatment of food animals?

Thus far most readers will agree with us, although strict vegans and most vegetarians will take issue with the idea that it is appropriate to use animals as food. We are on more difficult ground, however, when it comes to the use of animals in medical research, of which the use of animal models for genetic disease is one example. Arguing from a human-centred position and using a consequentialist approach, we might say that, provided no unnecessary suffering is imposed, the use of animals in this way is justified by the benefits for human health and welfare. What, it will be said, is wrong with sacrificing tens of thousands of mice if it saves the life of one child with cystic fibrosis? Indeed, certain US theologians, including Peters and Cole-Turner (reviewed by Deane-Drummond, 2001), have gone as far as to suggest that if this GM work brings benefits to humans it is wrong *not* to proceed with it.

There are many, however, Christians and non-Christians alike, who believe that the use of animals in medical research can never be justified by the results. They reject the consequentialist argument, believing that it is intrinsically wrong to impose suffering on non-human animals (or at least on some non-human animals: see below). Among Christian thinkers, Clark (1984) and Linzey (1987) reject the use of animals in experimental research or indeed as food. They suggest that knowledge of animals has increased and society has moved on since biblical times: we now recognize animals, if not as our equals, certainly as deserving of a high level of ethical consideration. The fact that our dentition and digestive physiology are adapted for a mixed diet is not regarded as relevant; in moral issues humankind can transcend nature. Linzey goes further by suggesting that animals are in some way indwelt by God's spirit and thus to use animals as commodities, whether as food or as experimental subjects, is an insult to the Creator (1993). Non-Christian thinkers such as Singer (1986, 1994) and Frey (2002) use the term 'speciesism' in describing attitudes which assume that humans are necessarily more ethically considerable than non-human animals, while both Linzey and the philosopher Regan (1983) speak of animal rights. Certainly the whole tenor of these authors' thinking is that we must not impose suffering on animals.

But many Christian thinkers have expressed reservations about these views. Barclay (1992) and Deane-Drummond (2001) both reject the notion of animal rights, since they can identify no corresponding animal responsibilities. Barclay in particular re-emphasizes the biblical position that humankind may make use of animals, with (as already noted) due provision for animal welfare. Barclay and de Pomerai (2002) also note that much of the writing on animal rights and similar issues is very selective, focusing almost entirely on mammals. Birds, which are also warm-blooded animals with complex nervous systems, are rarely mentioned[3] and even less attention is given to 'cold-blooded' vertebrates or to invertebrates[4] (see discussion by de Pomerai, 2002). The position taken by the latter two writers, and by the authors of this book, is that using animals for medical research is acceptable, provided there are clear benefits in the relief of human suffering. That is not to say, however, that animals may be used in medical research without any regard for their welfare. Statutory systems of licensing, inspection and review, which in the UK are established by Act of Parliament and implemented by the Home Office, are essential safeguards against the indiscriminate use of animals in such research (see Baggott la Velle, 2002b).

For those holding the latter position, genetic modification of animals would seem at first sight to present no new problems. In consequentialist terms, there seems little or no difference between genetically modifying pigs so that their organs can be used for human transplants and breeding pigs for pork and bacon, or between doing research with mice carrying human oncogenes and using mice for research on carcinogenic chemicals. However, the biologist-theologian Celia Deane-Drummond asks whether genetic modification of animals offends against their *telos*: their natural 'purposefulness', for which they were created. Does genetic modification of a sheep, for instance, deny its 'sheepness'? Certainly a sheep that produces a

---

3. Except in the context of factory farming of poultry; in the UK alone, about 850 million factory-farmed chickens are slaughtered each year for human consumption.

4. Several authors suggest that genetic proximity to humans affects the ethical status ascribed to animals.

human protein in its milk is making something that sheep do not naturally make. However, the sheep does not take on human attributes; it remains clearly a sheep, just as a bacterium making human insulin (Chapter 5) remains a bacterium. We thus argue that genetic modification of this type does not offend against the essential *telos* of the animal. We do, however, share Deane-Drummond's concerns about some of the more extreme results of 'conventional' animal-breeding, including the varieties of chicken and turkey used in factory farming and some varieties of domestic dogs. As we have already noted, these are clearly unable to perform many actions normal for their species (indeed, some varieties of dog are unable to breed without a good deal of help), suffer from a number of chronic conditions and, in the case of factory-farmed poultry, exhibit many of the symptoms of stress.

Thus we do not hold that GM per se presents any new ethical problems in relation to humankind's use of the animal kingdom. However, it is a different matter when we consider the possibility of genetically modifying humans.

Genetic modification of humans – general background

We have already shown that, despite the difficulties, genetic manipulation of mammals is possible and is established in medical research and biotechnology. Further, the combination of knowledge and experience in human cell biology, in embryology (including *in vitro* fertilization and culture of early embryos) and in human genetics (including the possibility of isolating and working with individual genes) sets the scene for the possible genetic manipulation of humans. Further still, the feasibility of applying these techniques to primates was demonstrated in 2001 by the genetic modification of a rhesus monkey (Vogel, 2001). Indeed, there were some who suggested that the latter event brought the advent of human genetic manipulation very much closer. We contest this view because, with our current state of knowledge, it would probably already be easier to produce a GM human than a GM monkey. What, then, is the current situation and what are the inherent and associated ethical and theological issues? Our discussion will deal with three topics: somatic cell gene therapy, germline gene therapy and genetic enhancement.

Somatic cell genetic modification and gene therapy

The term *somatic cell genetic modification* means changing the genetic make-up of cells in the body (*soma*) but not of the germline cells. Thus the genetic change is not inherited from generation to generation. It is used specifically in gene therapy, the treatment of a medical condition by genetic modification of cells or tissues in the patient, usually by directing the genes into the particular cells in which the medical condition is manifest. Thus in attempting to correct cystic fibrosis by this method, the 'normal' genes that are intended to supply the missing genetic function are directed at the lung's epithelial or lining cells. We need to state clearly, however, that at present, gene therapy is still very much in its early experimental stages. Early hopes that cystic fibrosis might be treatable by somatic cell gene therapy have not yet been fulfilled. Indeed, demonstrably successful treatments of genetic conditions have so far been very rare, although there has been a handful of successes with severe combined immunodeficiency disease (SCID) (reviewed by Turnpenny and Bryant, 2002). Even these successes, however, must be tempered by the news that some children treated for this condition have developed a white blood cell abnormality that may lead to leukaemia (Gore, 2003).

Ethically, somatic cell gene therapy appears in itself not to raise any new issues. There is, however, the more general issue of risk–benefit

---

Somatic cell gene therapy

- The correctly functioning gene is directed to the cells primarily affected by the genetic lesion: e.g. lung epithelium for cystic fibrosis, bone marrow for blood cell diseases.
- For most types of cell, repeated treatment is required. Stem cells such as bone marrow are exceptions to this.
- The success rate is currently very low.
- Depending on the specific technical details of the method used, the therapy carries varying and unquantifiable risks, e.g. the risk of activating oncogenes (genes that when active in the wrong place cause cancer).
- Side-effects such as abnormalities in the target cells may appear after treatment: e.g. abnormalities in white blood cells after bone-marrow gene therapy.
- Despite the risks, patients, or parents of child patients, usually wish to proceed because gene therapy may be the last hope.

---

analysis. These gene therapy treatments are essentially experimental, with low success rates, and they carry, to varying degrees, significant risk. In addition to the type of side effect mentioned in relation to SCID, there has been one fatality in the USA (see Smaglik, 2000a) that was directly attributable to the gene therapy treatment (and not to the disease against which the therapy was directed). However, adult patients and the parents of child patients have been quoted as saying that, experimental or not, risky or not, these treatments represent a last chance: the possibility, however remote, of success outweighs the risk.

Germline therapy

It is not currently permitted to modify humans genetically in the way that we have described for animals: that is, *heritable* genetic modification is forbidden. Thus, under the terms of the Human Fertilization and Embryology Act, although genetic modification of *in vitro* embryos is permitted for experimental purposes, those embryos must not be placed into the uterus of a prospective mother. The pragmatic reasons for this prohibition are easy to understand: there is still much uncertainty about the safety and possible side effects of manipulating human genomic DNA in a heritable manner. For example, the position effects referred to earlier mean that it is not possible to predict how active or effective the inserted gene will be in an individual. We are still a long way from solving this problem, as we noted in relation to non-human mammals. We observed, too, that there is the risk that the level of activity of the new gene may change in subsequent generations. Furthermore, there are concerns about the possible long-term consequences and hazards of germline therapy, which may persist over many generations. (As noted above, side effects are already known to occur in some somatic gene therapy treatments.) There is thus at present simply too much uncertainty about the irreversible perpetuation of genetic changes in succeeding generations for us to contemplate germline therapy.

Let us suppose, however, that gene therapy and genetic manipulation of the germline can be developed to become demonstrably and reproducibly safe, effective and workable. There are then likely to be pressures to use these techniques to *prevent* disease in future humans, especially where a family has already been affected. Indeed, whenever public attitudes are surveyed there is a clear majority who would approve of changing the genetic make-up of a future human for this purpose. The American theologian Ronald Cole-Turner (1993: 51) has thus written that the 'purpose of genetic engineering is to expand our ability to participate in God's work of redemption and creation and thereby to glorify God'. In this context of disease prevention, the Christian ethicist Robin Gill (1992) and the lawyer Sheila Dziobon (1999) have both argued, using a consequentialist approach, that germline therapy does not differ ethically from somatic cell therapy. We also hold this view, because successful germline therapy would lead to alleviation of suffering in subsequent generations. Further, as we have discussed previously (Bryant and Turnpenny, 2003), germline gene therapy represents to some a *higher* ethical standard than pre-implantation genetic diagnosis (PGD) or termination of pregnancy, in that it does not, in itself, involve the rejection of unsuitable embryos or abortion of foetuses. However, embryo selection (as in PGD) will almost certainly still be necessary in order to make sure that only embryos carrying the added DNA are implanted. The latter problem would be avoided if genetic manipulation of gametes could be successfully achieved, because most people do not ascribe to sperm and ova the status of 'life' that some ascribe to the early embryo (see Chapter 3).

Even if germline therapy is adopted as an acceptable technique, its use is likely to be limited. The reason for this is that in most cases it will be possible to select from several *in vitro* embryos those that will not be affected by the disease in question (see Chapter 6). The most probable use of germline gene therapy will be to supply a correctly functioning gene to embryos that are certain to be affected by genetic disease: for example, if both parents suffer from cystic fibrosis.

Some, however, take the view that, even if it would be needed only very rarely, human genetic engineering of the very early embryo will never be acceptable. First, there is still concern about the irreversible effects of manipulation for the succeeding lineage, even if the process itself has been shown to be safe for the individual who is the subject of the germline therapy. Secondly, as discussed in the context of pre-natal or pre-implantation genetic diagnosis, there is the issue of the acceptance of handicap and disability in society. If our stated aim is to reduce the incidence of genetically determined handicaps and disabilities, do we thereby imply that the handicapped and disabled have no value, or, if they have value, that it is very much inferior to that of those who are able in mind and body? The compassion of human society must surely be judged by its attitudes towards and its care of the sick, the vulnerable and the disadvantaged. Indeed, there is a consistent biblical imperative to care for the vulnerable and the weak. But the underlying tenets of medicine are to treat and prevent disease and to relieve suffering, tenets which also find parallels in biblical principles: there is a Christian mandate to heal, not least because it is a sign of God's kingdom. On this basis it may be justifiable to include genetic manipulation as a form of therapy in order to prevent handicap and disability, while at the same time acknowledging the worth of those judged to be handicapped and disabled. Thirdly, some will see germline therapy as a step too far in tampering with our own biological nature: the term 'playing God' is often used, but without necessarily any clear idea of what it actually means. Nevertheless, to those who accept germline therapy in principle it does indicate the need for wisdom in using this technology.

Genetic enhancement

For people who take a 'slippery slope' view of ethical thinking, permitting germline therapy will open the door to the use of genetic manipulation for the purposes of human enhancement. The concept of 'designer babies' is often raised in this context: parents choosing particular characteristics that they desire for their child and then ensuring, by genetic selection and/or manipulation of the embryo, that the child does indeed possess those characters. So, if it becomes possible to modify particular characters by genetic engineering, will there be a demand for it? This will depend to some extent on what characteristics or traits are on offer. Here we must distance ourselves from some of the pictures painted by the media. Sporting ability, artistic and musical talent and intelligence are all very complex characters influenced by many genes and by non-genetic factors. The idea that we could 'design' a runner in the mould of Paula Radcliffe, a cellist like Jacqueline du Pré or a mathematical genius like Albert Einstein is merely science fiction and is likely to remain so. Nevertheless, the possibility of manipulating simpler characters, such as eye or hair colour or even stature, is very real, and, even with a very limited range of choices, there are some who would opt for genetic enhancement (provided that they could afford it). The latter comment raises two more issues. First, it will not be cheap technology and its use is likely to be restricted on the basis of wealth. We return to this point below. Secondly, this is very, very unlikely to become available as mass technology; thus choices of parents are, despite the comments of some writers, equally unlikely to affect human genetic diversity.

Acceptable to some it may be, but does that make it right? The philosopher John Harris argues that if a particular feature in our child is important to us, then we should be able to choose it. For example, he says: 'If it is not wrong to hope for a bouncing, brown-eyed, curly-haired and bonny baby, can it be wrong to ensure that one has just such a baby? If it would not be wrong of God or Nature to grant such a wish, can it be wrong to grant it to oneself?' (Harris, 1998: 194). On the surface this sounds very plausible; but is it? In practice, couples who choose to have children accept and love them as they come. They hoped for a girl but it was a boy; they hoped for brown eyes but the baby is blue-eyed. The baby is still a gift from God.

Harris also suggests that if it becomes possible to provide the child with characteristics that give it a distinct advantage in life (that is to say, a greater advantage than might be effected by hair or eye colour), then that too will be acceptable. He posits that this is no different from buying advantage in education or in intensive sport or musical training: to Harris, these are simply outworkings of parents' wishes to give their child the best in life and the genetic version is no different ethically. This raises enormous issues that society has never properly faced up to in respect of equality of opportunity (genetic advantage will be available to the wealthy but not to the poor) and in respect of the value we place on individuals with differing abilities and backgrounds. Overall, we suggest that to choose specific genetically determined features is, albeit in a local, minor way, a form of eugenics, or at the very least of 'commodification': parents making their children into instruments of their wishes, meeting parental aspirations, rather than fully acknowledging children as individuals entitled to pursue their own potential and aspirations. Commodification certainly runs counter to Immanuel Kant's imperative that no human being should be treated as a means to an end. In relation to the New Testament, we suggest that it contravenes Jesus' second commandment (Matt. 22:39): to love our neighbours as ourselves. To use someone else, in this case a child, to meet one's own aspirations is not to treat that person as a neighbour.[5] We therefore draw a line ethically between germline genetic manipulation for therapeutic purposes and germline manipulation for enhancement. In this we are in agreement with most other Christian writers on this subject (see, for instance, the review of this topic in Peterson, 2001).

However, as we and other Christian writers have pointed out (Wyatt, 1998; Peterson, 2001; Song, 2002; Turnpenny and Bryant, 2002; Bryant and Turnpenny, 2003), it may be difficult to distinguish between treatment and enhancement. For example, in 'conventional' medicine, is limb-lengthening surgery, undertaken in order to make a young woman tall enough to become a flight attendant, treatment or enhancement? The same question may be asked in relation to surgery for breast enlargement and 'pure' cosmetic surgery. The problem here is that one person's enhancement is another person's treatment. For example, some may have psychological problems (and therefore need 'therapy') because of short stature while others do not. Self-image or body image, peer pressure and the cultural norms of a society are all important factors in determining individual perception of enhancement versus treatment.[6]

A further factor in comparing surgical enhancement with genetic enhancement is that in the former the person undergoing the surgery gives consent. For germline genetic enhancement, this is not possible: the subject of the enhancement is a very early embryo. Now, it can be argued, as indeed O'Donovan (1984) does, that all reproductive technologies involving embryos are done without consent. We suggest, however, that genetic enhancement of embryos differs from, for example, pre-implantation diagnosis in that enhancement involves changing the genetic make-up to meet parental aspirations without any consideration of what the wishes of the child might turn out to be (see above).

In the specific context of genetics, Peterson (2001) and Song (2002) discuss the therapy–enhancement distinction in some detail; readers who wish for a longer treatment of the subject are referred to

---

5. For a discussion of the very real dilemmas that arise when these ethical principles clash with other, equally valid ethically principles, see our discussion on donor embryos in Chapter 6.

6. In the UK, the Clothier Report (1991) rejected the use of genetic manipulation for 'cosmetic' reasons.

those authors. However, two examples from Song (2002: 74) further illustrate the dilemma. He quotes Daniels (1994), who defines as therapy any process that restores the person to the 'mean' or average position or to 'normal'. However, definition of the mean or the normal may be very difficult and thus the boundaries between therapy and enhancement are blurred. Jeungst (1997) has suggested that we may define therapy as being directed at specific genetic or physio-logical malfunctions, while enhancement is a change in a non-disease-causing genetic feature. Even this is not without its difficulties, however, as Song points out. How, for instance, would we regard a genetic modification that led to an increased resistance to viruses or bacteria ('genetic immunization')? According to Jeungst this may be therapy, but Daniels would regard it as elevating the individual above the norm and therefore to be classified as enhancement.

For many people, genetic enhancement through manipulation of embryos or gametes strikes at the very heart of an individual's autonomy, identity and dignity. Although this may be ascribing more to genes than is justified, this unease is certainly understandable and is clearly brought out in the 1998 *British Social Attitudes* survey. The survey gave evidence of strong support for genetic research and gene manipulation for the detection, prevention and treatment of *disease*, but there was little support for genetic *enhancement*. It will be interesting to see how public opinion will evolve as the technology is developed further. At present there is no justification for assuming that human genetic research is leading steadily and inexorably towards 'designer babies'; there is no indication at present that this is generally acceptable to scientists, clinicians or the public, even if there are some individuals in all of those groups who would be comfortable with such developments. Nevertheless, it is important that the ethical debate remains vigorous, keeping pace with scientific progress and seeking broad views through public consultation. In dealing with this type of issue, it is good to be ethically prepared rather than being caught unawares. We need to be wise before the event.

8. UNLOCKING GENETIC POTENTIAL: CLONING AND STEM-CELL TECHNOLOGY

Male and female he created them.
(Gen. 1:27b)

For in him we live and move and have our being ... We are his offspring.
(Acts 17:28)

Clones are fun!
(Richard Seed)

In whose image?

Hello, Dolly

The 27 February 1997 edition of the prestigious science journal *Nature* contained an unexciting-sounding paper, 'Viable offspring derived from fetal and adult mammalian cells' (Wilmut et al., 1997). And yet, to those in the know, this typically British understatement represented a very significant step in our understanding of the development of mammals. Indeed, it was significant enough to have been included in *Nature*'s press release for that week and thus to cause media interest of an intensity that biologists had never encountered before. What was the fuss about? The sheep described in the paper, Dolly, was a genetic copy – a *clone* – of an adult sheep and had been born at the Roslin Institute, Edinburgh, as a result not of a conventional fertilization but of a transfer of the genetic material from an adult cell (from a valuable GM ewe) to an *oocyte* (egg cell) from which the genetic material had been removed. In other words, the two sets of chromosomes that Dolly possessed came not from *two* parents but from *one*. The technical term employed for this procedure is cloning by *somatic cell nuclear transfer* (Figure 8.1).

The significance placed on this depended very much on one's viewpoint. For developmental biologists it illustrated a feature that

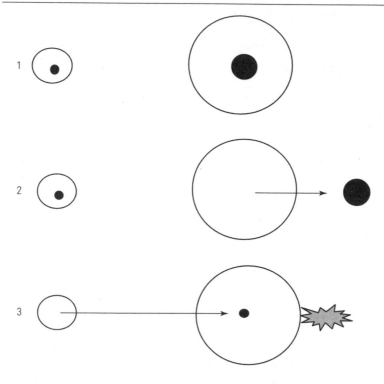

1. An adult cell at the left and an egg cell (oocyte) at the right. The DNA of both cells is contained in a structure called the nucleus, represented by the solid black circles. The adult cell contains two sets of DNA; the unfertilized egg contains one.

2. The nucleus is removed from the egg cell.

3. The egg cell nucleus is replaced with a nucleus from the adult cell. The new cell-nucleus combination is stimulated to divide (as a normally fertilized egg would do), often by a very brief electric shock. If an embryo is formed it is placed in the womb in order to establish a pregnancy. It will be a genetic copy of the adult from which the nucleus (containing the DNA) was obtained.

Figure 8.1. Illustration of the basic cloning procedure

had been shown for plants and for certain animals, including frogs, over forty years earlier. This was the demonstration that adult cells retain the genetic information present in the newly fertilized egg: that is, in scientific terminology, they are *totipotent*. Although this had been readily demonstrated by study of the genes themselves, no-one had previously been able to achieve in mammalian cells the re-programming of the genes, so that they could start again at the beginning of the developmental process. The magnitude of this achievement, however, has been overshadowed by the significance placed by the media and by many non-scientists on the fact that Dolly was a clone. Much of the debate centred on the possibility that the cloning technique might be applied to humans. On that basis, the Pope condemned cloning outright; in the USA, President Bill Clinton requested that his Bioethics Advisory Committee should report on cloning as a matter of urgency. That report, published in June 1997, recommended a moratorium on the use of government funds for research on cloning. (Under the subsequent presidency of George Bush Jr, a total ban on human cloning was incorporated in law by the Human Cloning Prohibition Act of 2001.) The World Health Organization and UNESCO both passed resolutions recommending the prohibition of human cloning, on the basis that it would be an affront to human dignity and a violation of human rights. The Council of Europe expressed similar views, as did the UK's Royal Society (see Griffin, 2002). In the UK, the cloning of humans was made unlawful by Act of Parliament at the beginning of 2002.

However, although the cloning of Dolly generated much negative comment in the media, in national and international organizations and among the public, there were some who clearly welcomed these developments, again for reasons unconnected with the implications for biological science and biotechnology. Thus one distinguished scientific author is reported as saying that he would like to clone himself, while a correspondent to the *Guardian* newspaper stated that she wanted to clone her father so that she could cradle him as a baby in her arms. Some parents of children with terminal illnesses talked about replacing the child by cloning; several actually approached the Roslin Institute asking for help with this (Wellcome Trust, 1998). Thinking along the lines of 'copying' specific people had been predicted in Fay Weldon's novel *The Cloning of Joanna May*, in which a man arranges that while his wife, Joanna May, is undergoing surgery, cells are removed to be used as sources of DNA in order to clone her, thus providing, in the future, 'new' versions of Joanna. The idea that one can clone a specific person with all their individual characteristics is based on the absolute genetic determinist/ reductionist philosophy that we discussed in Chapters 3 and 6. There is no need to repeat the earlier discussion at length, but we need to restate that, even at the physical level, the genetic clone will differ from the adult from which the genes were obtained because of differing effects of environment, starting inside the uterus. Indeed, genetically identical twins may in some cases not look identical. It will also be impossible to mimic the factors that influence emotional, social and spiritual development. The clone of that woman's father would not be her father because he would not have the experience of being her father. As Dr Frank Burnett, a former editor of *The Biochemist*, put it so well in his series *Science on the Buses*, we have no way of knowing whether a clone of a great dictator will become a Hitler or a Charlie Chaplin. Nevertheless, there are some biomedical scientists who seem determined to press ahead with attempts to produce a human by cloning (see also Chapter 9).

Genotypes to order?

Before discussing the ethical and theological aspects of human cloning, we must remind ourselves that mammalian (including human) genetic clones occur in nature. Such clones are, of course, identical or monozygotic twins; they occur as a result of splitting of the early embryo (see discussion in Chapter 3). Indeed, in the breeding of valuable cattle, embryos 'rescued' from the fallopian tubes after fertilization or created by *in vitro* fertilization are often deliberately split in order to increase the numbers of animals that are born. Such a procedure would be entirely feasible for human embryos created by *in vitro* fertilization but, in the UK at least, the Human Fertilization and Embryology Act 1990 forbids the deliberate twinning of embryos for subsequent implantation into a woman's uterus. The Act also forbids the implantation of genetically modified embryos; after the announcement of the birth of Dolly there was some discussion about whether using genetic material from an adult cell to initiate development could be regarded as genetic modification. There were suggestions that this might represent a loophole in the legal provision, through which human cloning might slip, but in fact the Act is interpreted as prohibiting the implantation of cloned embryos.

Risky procedures

As mentioned already, if it is possible to clone other mammals it is in theory possible to clone humans. One of the key questions raised by this possibility is: 'Is it safe to do so?' In answering this question we need to remind ourselves that cloning is not yet a 'routine' procedure. In the experimentation leading to the birth of Dolly, 430 oocytes (egg cells) were collected from hormonally treated ewes, from which 277 early 'embryos' were created. Only twenty-nine of these developed normally to the blastocyst stage (see Chapter 3); these were implanted in thirteen surrogate mothers, but only one successful pregnancy ensued (Griffin, 2002). Seven years on, there is still a strong empirical element, even though re-programming of adult DNA in order to create clones has been extended to several other mammalian species and exhibits a much higher general success rate now than in early 1997. For each species, the particular conditions need to be worked out, including donation of oocytes, treatment of the oocytes, optimization of donor cell selection, formation of experimental embryos, experimental implantations and the establishment of experimental pregnancies. The excellent and informative website of the Roslin Institute, <www.roslin.ac.uk/public/cloning.html>, carries a frequently updated summary of progress with mammalian cloning. Live-birth rates from initial attempts at creating embryos are mostly around 1%, although rates as high as 5% for cattle, 6% for mice and 7% for goats have been achieved in particular laboratories.

This is very relevant to application of this procedure to humans. Attempting to clone humans at this stage in the development of the subject would be to treat humans, and women in particular, as experimental objects. Whatever our attitude is to cloning per se (and this is discussed below), the 'state of the art' must influence our thinking on the matter. To set out to clone an individual human would first require women willing to donate oocytes from which the nucleus would be removed in order to receive the genetic material from a donor (as shown earlier, in Figure 8.1). Secondly, it would require many women to be willing to act as surrogate mothers knowing that there was a high probability that they would experience the spontaneous abortion of a malformed embryo or – perhaps worse – bringing to term a seriously malformed embryo. Most people regard using humans as purely experimental material in this way as being both intrinsically wrong and abhorrent.[1] Indeed, scientists at the Roslin Institute have opposed the idea of human cloning on these grounds (see Griffin, 2002). Furthermore, conventional medical ethics provides for evaluation of experimental procedures in terms of risk versus benefit to the patient (see e.g. Jones, 2002) and, on this

---

1. Note that, as discussed in Chapter 2, abhorrence does not necessarily relate to rightness or wrongness.

basis alone, attempts to clone a human are currently unacceptable. Using humans in experiments of this type is to deny their dignity as individuals and to use them in a singularly instrumental manner. Christians will add that such an approach falls far short of loving other people as we love ourselves and of treating every other human as being made in God's image.

Nevertheless, we concede that experimental procedures do take place in the practice of medicine, often in the form of testing new treatments. Provided that benefit is possible and the person to be subjected to the experimental procedure has given informed consent, then ethics committees will permit such procedures. In countries where cloning of humans is illegal, including the UK, informed consent is not relevant; cloning is simply not permitted. In countries where cloning is permitted, however, informed consent of the individual may be the key issue. In such cases, we would argue, 'informed' must mean being informed of all the risks. We further add that, at present at least, we do not believe that the risks are justified by the benefits, especially if the cloning has been undertaken to satisfy curiosity.

New ethics or old?
Let us, however, now look into the future. Let us suppose that, for whatever reason, experiments on mammalian cloning have continued and that the success rate is as high as for live births after *in vitro* fertilization. Let us further suppose that there are indications that the techniques will work equally well with higher primates. In other words, it would be entirely feasible to go about creating a genetic clone of an individual human with a real chance of success, with odds favourable enough for a potential surrogate mother to find the risk acceptable. This focuses our attention on whether it is ethical to clone a human. That focus has been made more acute by the recent claims from South Korea and from Italy that pregnancies had been established with cloned embryos. There were sensational claims in late 2002 and in 2003 from a company called Clonaid, working with a bizarre Canadian pseudo-religious sect, the Raelians, that its cloning techniques had resulted in the birth of five human clones. However, no-one has been allowed to test the DNA of the mothers and the children in order to verify the claim, which is widely regarded as a hoax and/or a publicity stunt in very bad taste.

There are some writers, including the philosopher John Harris (1997; Burley and Harris, 1999) and the Chicago scientist Richard Seed (1999), who suggest that there are no intrinsic ethical objections to human cloning. Severino Antinori and his team in Italy, who claim to have established a pregnancy with a cloned human embryo, presumably think similarly. There is even a hint of this line of thought among some Christian writers (Cole-Turner, 1997). At the other end of the scale, conservative Roman Catholics object to reproductive cloning for the same reason that they oppose *in vitro* fertilization: namely, that it separates sexual activity from procreation. They also have objections to IVF, as do some conservative evangelicals, based on a very high view of the status of pre-implantation embryos, arguing that it is not ethically acceptable either to use them in experiments or to dispose of 'spare' embryos (see e.g. George, 2001; P. Taylor, 2002). We have already discussed the status of the pre-implantation embryo in Chapter 3, noting that UK law, as set out in the Human Fertilization and Embryology Act, allows the creation of embryos that are surplus to those needed for insertion into the uterus; it also allows experimentation on *in vitro* embryos for diagnostic and therapeutic purposes, as well as the disposal of surplus embryos including those that have been used in experiments. For society in general, although not for all Christians, it appears that the status of the *in vitro* embryo is not an issue in an ethical discussion of cloning. Indeed, one Christian writer (Jones, 2002), in urging a rational debate among Christians, suggests that it is possible to regard reproductive cloning as being simply at one end of a range of reproductive technologies which also includes donor insemination, IVF and pre-implantation genetic diagnosis. This is not to deny the possibility that cloning may raise particular ethical issues, but does, in Jones's view, place cloning in an appropriate medical context.

Are there then specific ethical issues that are raised by cloning humans? We need to acknowledge that some of the ethical debate, both in 1997 and subsequently, has expressed a repugnance (the 'yuk' factor) at the very idea of cloning humans. For some, it represented a further step along a path of *in vitro* reproductive technologies that should not have been taken in the first place (thus in fact agreeing with Jones, 2002, that cloning is simply one end of the spectrum of such technologies). One influential ethicist who expresses such repugnance is the current chair of President Bush's advisory committee on stem-cell research, Leon Kass. He is well known for his antagonism to *in vitro* fertilization, and his opposition to cloning, clearly expressed in his essay 'The Wisdom of Repugnance' (Kass, 1998), is set in that context. However, much of the more generally expressed repugnance, for example in newspaper correspondence columns, media debates and web-based discussion forums, was not based on a general rejection of reproductive technologies but was a repugnant reaction specifically to cloning. The public consultation carried out by the Wellcome Trust (1998) revealed that such views were held very widely, often coupled with worries about the disruption of family relationships. In reporting these views, the Wellcome Trust uses the words of Kass (1998) to state that many members of the public view human cloning as 'a blatant violation of the inner meaning of parent–child relations'. We have argued elsewhere (Chapter 2; Bryant et al., 2002) that repugnance per se is not a safe basis for moral decision-making although, with Midgley (2000), we recognize that it may have its basis in deeply held religious and/or cultural values. We note also that many procedures that are now widely (although not necessarily universally) acceptable were greeted with moral repugnance when they were first announced. These procedures include organ transplants, especially heart transplants, donor insemination, and *in vitro* fertilization.

Turning now to more 'formal' ethical discussion, it is helpful to think of what possible reason there may be for cloning a human. Some of the earlier enthusiastic and positive responses to the possibility of cloning humans were based on the motivation of re-creating a specific person such as a loved one, or indeed individuals themselves. The error of this idea has already been dealt with: a clone will reproduce a genotype (i.e. a specific set of genes), with no guarantee of how that clone will turn out as a person. Our personhood relies on very much more than our genes. Indeed, as both Messer (2001) and Jones (2002) have already stated so well, our personhood and identity are gifts from God: we cannot manufacture them by copying a particular genotype. (Readers wishing for a fuller treatment of this are referred back to Chapters 3 and 6.) However, because the genetic material used to create a cloned embryo is taken from a cell in an adult, the experimenter does have a good idea of how the genotype will be translated into the physical phenotype – in other words, how it will 'turn out' physically. With the caveat that even this aspect of development is subject to environmental influences, again including the uterine environment, for some people this might provide enough incentive to try.

As a side issue, not directly relevant to the ethics of cloning per se, but certainly relevant to public perceptions, we need to emphasize here that cloning is not mass technology. In the light of the biomedical community's forty-plus years' experience of cloning frogs and twenty-five years of experience of human *in vitro* fertilization, it is very unlikely to become so. We are therefore not talking about creating armies of drones to carry out menial jobs, or of growing a football team. The film *The Boys from Brazil* is often cited in these discussions, but it is highly unrealistic.[2] Nevertheless it is clearly possible to think of reproducing a specific genotype with desirable characteristics.

This brings us to the topic of eugenics: the selection of favoured genotypes, with the corollary that other genotypes are not so desirable. Although this was discussed in Chapter 7, it is worth restating here that any form of genetic discrimination contravenes the autonomy and dignity of individual humans (standards to which Christians, and those of other faiths or no faith at all, widely subscribe) and treats some humans as being of less worth than others. Again this runs counter to the Christian view of humankind, in which each individual is both our neighbour (actually or potentially) whom we should love and whom God does love. Further, those who are favoured by the discrimination and therefore, in the current context, may be cloned, are also being treated as commodities, their clones being created specifically in an attempt to fulfil the wishes of someone else. Whatever one thinks about treating the rest of the living world in this way (for instance, farm animals), treating another human as a commodity – that is, in a specifically instrumental way – is wrong.

There is, however, another element in this debate, as exemplified by two television programmes broadcast on UK channels (Westcountry TV, 1999; BBC TV, 1999). In both programmes it was suggested that an acceptable use of cloning was to have a child if all other routes, including 'conventional' IVF, were not possible. The suggestion was supported in each programme by interviews with

---

2. The film, made as long ago as 1978, places the notorious Nazi Dr Joseph Mengele in South America, where he engages in cloning a small army of very Aryan-looking neo-Nazis. Equally unrealistic are the scenarios that envisage cloning extinct animals from fragments of DNA. *Jurassic Park* is great fun but pure science fiction, whatever Steven Spielberg said about science fact!

articulate and intelligent married couples who were in just such a situation. At least, they argued, the child who would be conceived by this method would carry the genes of one parent (and would of course be of the same sex): namely, the parent who had donated the nucleus. Since then a number of lesbian couples have suggested that cloning may be an acceptable way for them to produce a child, rather than having to use donor insemination (as predicted by fictional scenarios in the public consultation undertaken by the Wellcome Trust, 1998). These suggestions clearly support Jones's comment that cloning may be regarded as just another reproductive technology (Jones, 2002). But are there specific ethical responses to this?

An argument often raised is that of a 'right to a child'. Fundamental to this argument is that infertility or sub-fertility are thought of as pathological conditions that demand medical intervention. Indeed, Harris (1997) would permit cloning on the grounds of reproductive rights or what he calls 'procreative autonomy'. It is certainly true that for those who want children the inability to produce them causes great distress (Snowden and Snowden, 1993; Baggott la Velle, 2002a), a distress that we also see recorded in the Old and New Testament Scriptures in relation to wives, such as Sarah, Hannah and Elizabeth, who were 'barren'. We do not believe, however, that is helpful to think of having a child as a basic human right, even though we recognize the very strong drive in many people to reproduce (cf. Baggott la Velle, 2002a). Indeed, those 'barren' women whose distress is recorded in the Bible regarded a child as a gift from God and pleaded with God that he should bestow that gift. In our society, we suggest that it is an appropriate use of God-given talents to use advances in medical science in order to help those who have difficulty in conceiving, as in the development of IVF. But if a child is a divine gift we cannot demand to have one.

However, the couples interviewed for the television programmes were not suitable candidates for 'conventional' IVF. They were very clear in their arguments. They could not have children; cloning might help them to have children; this is a good use of cloning; therefore cloning is acceptable. This is a very consequentialist view. Indeed, on a local scale it is utilitarian, increasing the sum of human happiness at least as far as these couples are concerned. But is there an alternative, perhaps a Christian, view? First, an acceptance of reproductive cloning for otherwise childless couples goes a long way along the road of regarding a child as a right to be had at any price and by any couple, including lesbian couples, rather than as a precious gift from God, even given that we already use interventive technology to help some couples to conceive. Secondly, God has created humans as beings that reproduce sexually. We are not referring here to the act of sexual intercourse, but rather to the coming together of gametes (eggs and sperm) of different genetic make-up, thereby creating a new genetic mix that is such a wonder to parents. *In vitro* fertilization techniques, although they separate the act of sexual intercourse from the process of procreation, preserve this coming together of the genetic material from the two parents. We do not hold naturalness or unnaturalness as in themselves being strong factors in the ethical argument, but it is surely relevant to our consideration here that cloning is so very different biologically from the system that God has created. Indeed, it may be a wise or virtuous view to hold that cloning is a step too far in the applications of biomedical science. Although in general we do not recognize the distinction made by O'Donovan (1984) between 'begetting' and 'making' in respect of *in vitro* technologies, reproductive cloning may be the one clear example of that distinction.[3]

It is also important to consider the children themselves who may be born via these cloning procedures. Would their unconventional origin have any psychological effects? We cannot predict an answer to this. For people produced by cloning, the genetic mother and father would of course be one generation further back than in normal sexual union; the clone would not arise from a conventional or even an *in vitro* fertilization and would not therefore have a mother and father in the biological sense, at least in the way in which we normally use those terms. Knowledge of this fact might be disturbing. Further, the clone will have been created specifically to fulfil the wishes of others and may experience ongoing pressure so to do. Again, as argued clearly by Burley and Harris (1999), these consequentialist arguments are not specific to cloning. Such pressure is applied by some parents who have specific expectations for their naturally produced children (see also Chapter 7). When those expectations are not met, it can

---

3. O'Donovan's position is that 'begetting' via 'natural' fertilization, conception and childbirth brings into the world beings like ourselves. 'Making', on the other hand, involving 'unnatural' procedures in the laboratory or clinic, including IVF, brings into the world beings that are not like ourselves. We cannot support this view in general, although there is some justification for it in respect of cloning.

lead to feelings of disappointment in the parents and of failure in the child. These feelings may well contribute to poor relationships in the family and in the adult life of the child. These difficulties are likely to be more intense if the child was produced by cloning to meet specific parental expectations.

Even if the clone had been brought into being simply as means of having a child when all else had failed, looking uncannily like a younger version of one's mother or father would draw constant attention to the rather unusual origin of the individual. We further believe that there may be specific dangers in this. Having a daughter who grew up to look very similar indeed to the way her mother looked twenty-five or thirty years previously might well be a serious sexual temptation to a father.

Overall, therefore, there are potentially serious and possibly unresolvable problems relating to the mental and emotional health of humans produced by cloning. Although these may not be intrinsic to cloning per se, we suggest that a wise or virtuous Christian response should be to refrain from undertaking a process that generates such difficulties.

The image of God

Lastly, it is necessary to consider the status of a clone in the sight of God. Of course, we get no specific illumination of this problem from Scripture. There is absolutely no reason to suppose, however, that being identical genetically to someone else excludes a person from the love of God. We do not believe that identical twins are only half persons because they have identical sets of genes; nor is there any indication that identical twins are in some way inferior in God's sight. Indeed, we might wonder what sort of God it was who might discriminate in this way. It is clear from the Bible that God's love extends in general to all humankind and in particular to all who will receive it. However, in respect of cloned humans, Gina Kolata (1998) has suggested that in cloning we may be 'forcing God to give us another soul' or, even worse, 'creating soul-less beings ... genetic shells of humans'. Even without the strong element of Hellenistic dualism[4] apparent in this statement, surely this does not accord with

---

4. The idea that a human is two separate entities, a body and a soul; this contrasts with the biblical view of the wholeness of human persons: integrated beings of body, mind and spirit.

a biblical view of God? So, although there may be ethical objections to human cloning, we suggest that it is inconceivable that a person born as a genetic clone of a pre-existing adult should be regarded as any less of a person, of being any less in God's image, or of being any less an object of God's love than are people who are the result of a normal genetic union.

Cloning

- May damage the future physical health, psychological well-being and family relationships of the clone
- Raises questions about the status of the pre-implantation embryo
- May be used for the promotion of so-called desirable human characteristics and the devaluing of others
- Treats human beings as a commodity
- Prevents the natural process of genetic mixing in human procreation, upon which the wonder of conceiving, bearing and nurturing children depend

---

New cells for old – stem cells and spare parts

The perfect match: 'Therapeutic cloning'

We now turn to consider 'therapeutic' cloning. This refers to the idea of using cloning as a means of generating 'spare' body parts. The idea is based on the fact that a few days after fertilization the embryo has become a hollow sphere, the blastocyst, in which the cells destined to become placenta begin to be distinguishable from those that will become the embryo proper. At this stage, we can identify *stem cells*: cells that have the developmental potential to form many different types of cell. Developmental biologists have had some success in persuading these embryonic stem cells to grow into particular types of cell in the laboratory (see Pederson, 1999). Indeed, this work was awarded the title of 'Breakthrough of the Year, 1999' by the top-line American journal *Science*. The possibility is thus raised that embryonic stem cells may be a source of tissues and even organs. Further, using embryos generated by nuclear replacement cloning can offer a significant advantage. Suppose that a person needs or is likely to need a tissue graft or replacement of an organ because of the effects of serious damage caused by disease or accident. The proposed scenario is that a nucleus from one of that person's cells would be used to initiate an embryo, as in reproductive cloning. However, instead of being intended for eventual insertion into a uterus, this embryo would be intended as source of stem cells. Any tissues or organs grown from those stem cells would be immunologically compatible with the original donor of the genetic material that initiated the clone (i.e. the patient). Thus problems of tissue rejection would be avoided.

Although personalized spare parts may at present seem a little far-fetched, this use of cloning is both medically and scientifically plausible, although not in the immediate future. Several laboratories are working on the development of the use of embryonic stem cells in this way, albeit mostly with model systems such as mouse embryos created by IVF. However, one commercially funded laboratory in the USA has reported the generation of eight human blastocysts after somatic cell nuclear transfer (Cibelli et al., 2001), although the report has been greeted with scepticism by some other scientists, but the report from a joint USA–Korean team of the creation of thirty blastocysts early in 2004 (Hwang et al., 2004) is rather better substantiated. We should add that, under recent legislation, this research is now illegal in federally funded laboratories in the USA (see below), but not in South Korea.

Does this raise any new ethical issues? Certainly those people who base their objections to IVF and to reproductive cloning on their views of the status of the early embryo will also object to this. They will point out, with some justification, that research is also proceeding on use of adult stem cells, such as those from bone marrow, to generate a range of cells and tissues (see also 'What's ethics got to do with it?' below). But what of those who accept the legal status of the early embryo as defined by the HFE Act? Certainly the Wellcome Trust's public consultation (Wellcome Trust, 1998) found that in general there was little opposition to therapeutic cloning, although there was a desire to be reassured that research along these lines would bring definite benefits to humans. Clearly the prime mode of ethical thinking was a utilitarian one. Whether individual Christians will go along with this viewpoint will depend on many factors but, if appropriate, we should not be afraid to express clearly thought-out views that run counter to general public opinion.

Back to basics: Stem-cell research
Even though the advantages for generating matched tissues by therapeutic cloning are readily apparent, it must be emphasized that

obtaining a blastocyst after somatic cell nuclear transfer into an egg cell is not yet a routine procedure. It may in the future become so, but for the present it cannot be regarded as a straightforward route to generating tissues and/or organs as matched 'spare parts'. For this reason, the focus has transferred to research on stem cells from embryos generated by 'conventional' *in vitro* fertilization. The basic rationale is the same as that described above for therapeutic cloning, except that the 'spare parts' do not come with a built-in tissue match. In terms of numbers a supply of embryos for this research is not at present a problem: many extra embryos are generated during IVF procedures, although up to 2001 only 108 had been generated specifically for use in research (Griffin, 2002). In view of the spare embryos created in IVF, the Princeton-based, strongly anti-Christian philosopher and bioethicist Peter Singer has suggested that stem-cell research would be an appropriate use for them. However, this type of research is now banned in the USA, at least in federally funded institutions, under the provisions of the Prohibition of Human Cloning Act of 2001, a position which is supported by many Christians.

What's ethics got to do with it?
In the UK there is no ban on stem-cell research. As the potential of such research became apparent in the late 1990s, the UK government asked its Chief Medical Officer, Professor Liam Donaldson, to convene a group of experts to look at the topic. The Donaldson Report was published in 2000 and recommended that the Human Fertilization and Embryology Act 1990 be amended to allow the creation of embryos specifically for the generation of stem cells. The amendment to the Act was passed in both Houses of Parliament in late 2000 and early 2001 and is now incorporated into the code of practice under which the HFEA operates. It is the view of the chair of the Parliamentary Select Committee on Science and Technology, Dr Ian Gibson MP, that this change to the Act has stimulated research in the UK, which, he believes, now has a leading position in this research. We note here that several other EU countries are in a position to change their laws on research on *in vitro* embryos in a similar way.

Interestingly, there was little public debate prior to the parliamentary votes, although members of both Houses were lobbied on the one hand by (mainly) Christian organizations, such as Christian

Stem cells

- Stem cells are cells that can develop into many different cell types.
- For example, bone-marrow cells give rise to all the different types of blood cells.
- Stem cells that occur in the early embryo have the potential to develop into *all* the different types of cell found in the body. Because of this they are described as *totipotent*.
- Stem cells that occur in a developed body, whether infant or adult, have a more limited potential – they give rise to a more limited range of cells, such as blood cells. They are therefore described as *pluripotent*.
- Research is in progress aimed at using stem cells in repair of damaged tissues and organs; i.e. to grow 'spare parts'.
- Because embryonic stem cells are totipotent, they are regarded as the best source of stem cells.
- Embryos for stem cells may be created by cloning techniques, or more likely by *in vitro* fertilization (the latter process creates spare embryos).
- This raises questions about the ethical status of the early embryo and about commodification of embryos.
- There is also active research into the possibility of widening the developmental potential of adult stem cells.

Action Research and Education and the Roman Catholic Church, that oppose any experimentation on embryos (P. Taylor, 2002; George, 2001) and on the other by various patient groups that wanted the research to be permitted and to proceed as fast as possible. Their arguments were essentially that this research would help sick and injured people, so it must be allowed to go ahead. Among the latter groups there was little discussion of the status of the embryo, and among the wider public even less. This is perhaps not surprising, since the creation of human embryos for reproduction and for research under licence has been widely accepted in the UK.

The same is not true in the USA, where the banning of stem-cell research was to a large extent based on conservative views of the status of the pre-implantation embryo. The actor Christopher Reeve, who formerly played Superman but is now very extensively paralysed after a riding accident, has a personal interest in the possibility of regenerating nervous tissue from stem cells. He has entered vociferously into the debate in the USA and is reported as saying, 'Bigots are delaying my recovery' (Reeve, 2002). By 'bigots' he actually means those who hold that the early embryo should be afforded full human status. He then goes on to discuss in some detail the alternative view of the early embryo (set out in Chapter 3), including some interesting social insights, before reaching his conclusion that stem-cell research not only should be permitted but should be encouraged. But we suppose that, given his condition, 'He would say that, wouldn't he?'

By now it will be apparent that the ethical discussion has proceeded along two different lines. A minority (at least in the UK), taking the view that the early human embryo is a human person, have raised intrinsic objections to the research because to them it is research on humans. The majority have taken an essentially consequentialist or utilitarian line: if the research will bring benefits it should be done.

In Chapter 3 we made it clear that, although we respect the views of those who regard the early embryo as a human person, we do not believe that this position is scientifically or medically tenable, or that it is reliably supported by Scripture. It might be supposed, then, that those holding this latter view would be entirely happy with stem-cell research based on human embryos *in vitro*. Certainly some are, but others, including many Christians, wish to take a more circumspect line, as follows.

An embryo created for the specific purpose of providing stem cells is never intended for insertion into the uterus; it is not regarded as a potential human. Embryos created by IVF or even, some day in the future, by cloning (albeit with all the objections mentioned), are actually intended as future humans and are treated as such until the surplus ones are discarded. (As discussed in Chapter 3, even the latter process in some ways mimics the wastage of early embryos that occurs in nature.) However, the creation of embryos just to make spare parts treats them in a purely instrumental way: it results in their commodification. Does this not run counter to the wishes of the Warnock Committee (Warnock, 1985), the recommendations of which were the basis for the HFE Act? Although the committee members did not view the pre-implantation embryo as a human person, neither did they regard it as morally inconsiderable; they were clear that society does not have *carte blanche* in respect of the treatment of such embryos. Indeed, in the vote in the House of Lords, Mary Warnock herself voted against amending the HFE Act, on the grounds that it would turn human embryos into commodities, and she was criticized in the press for so doing. In fact, as she stated in an interview, she has subsequently changed her mind, not as a result of the press criticism but following further reflection and discussion.

Be that as it may, it is probable that many readers of this book have sympathy with Mary Warnock's original position. They would thus urge restraint in the use of *in vitro* embryos for generating stem cells, perhaps pointing out that success was now being achieved in the re-programming of adult stem cells,[5] research that shared the award for 'Breakthrough of the Year, 1999' mentioned earlier. This 'intermediate' ethical position steers away from the deontological prohibition of the use of embryos in stem-cell research and also from the purely consequentialist position that justifies the research on the grounds that it may lead to benefit. This is in fact a wisdom-based or virtue-based ethical position, very similar to that developed in the writing of the biologist-theologian Celia Deane-Drummond (e.g. Deane-Drummond, 2001).

Is such a position logically tenable? Certainly it cannot be argued from either a purely deontological or a purely consequentialist position. Yet it clearly has its merits: it moves us away from formulaic approaches to what is a difficult problem and asks what is wise or virtuous. An approach based on wisdom or virtue may not in the end lead to a prohibition of using embryos for the generation of stem cells, but even if not, it may give time for thought and reflection (for Christians, prayerful reflection). And where do we, the authors, stand on this? Based on the views of the status of the early embryo (see Chapter 3), one of us believes that experimentation of this type is acceptable while the other, with the same view of the status of the early embryo, is nevertheless concerned about the commodification of the embryo. As we have seen so often in this book, there is no clear 'Christian view'; we again pray for love and harmony among those who reach different conclusions.

---

5. Embryonic stem cells are *totipotent*, having the potential to develop into all the 200-plus cell types in the body. Adult stem cells are *pluripotent*, having the ability to develop into a limited range of cell types. For example, bone-marrow stem cells give rise to all the different types of blood cell. It is a challenge for developmental biologists to manipulate adult stem cells so that their developmental potential is broadened.

9. TO BOLDLY GO?

For the LORD gives wisdom,
  and from his mouth come knowledge and understanding.

Then you will understand what is right and just
  and fair – every good path.
(Prov. 2:6, 9)

The future isn't what it used to be.
(Walter Truett Anderson)[1]

Introduction

'Be prepared.' So says the motto of the Boy Scout movement. But are Christians prepared adequately for the ethical debate about genetics, cloning and related issues? Writing in 1999, Audrey Chapman[2] suggested that the answer then was 'No.' Her case was essentially that, for the most part, Christians had failed to engage with and debate the 'new biology' and its implications for human society. We may feel this to be rather harsh, since in the same book she acknowledged that some theologians on both sides of the Atlantic had contributed usefully to the debate and that there had been several publications from groups set up by churches or by inter-church organizations at the institutional level. This work by theologians, ethicists and Christian groups has continued since 1999. Nevertheless, there remains a challenge in what Chapman has argued. The new biology of which we have written here has the potential to affect the lives of very many human beings, perhaps even ourselves and our families. It is thus appropriate that Christian minds are brought to bear on these subjects, not only at the level of the institutional church, not

---

1. From the World Future Society website, <www.wfs.org/wfs>, 2001.

2. The Revd Dr Audrey Chapman is an ordained Christian minister and Director of the Program of Dialogue on Science, Ethics and Religion at the American Association for the Advancement of Science (Washington, DC).

only involving theological 'experts', but at the level of the local church, including local groups and individuals. It is our experience that increasingly this is happening. It is our hope that this volume (and the lectures on which it is based) will have helped to inform that interest.

However, the science is not static. It is moving at great pace: what we thought of as improbable yesterday may tomorrow become routine. We therefore now identify some of the directions in which the science and its applications are moving. Much of the interest, of course, lies in human biology and so, after a brief excursion into the fields to look at GM crops, we focus almost entirely on the applications that may affect individual humans. In general we note that as the background science advances, so the possible technical applications become more sophisticated and the pressure for more wide-ranging applications grows. This does not necessarily throw up any new ethical challenges, but it will certainly increase the intensity and the urgency with which these challenges will have to be addressed. So, what does the future hold?

Where are we going?

GM crops

The main scientific feature to note here is that our knowledge of plant genes and their control mechanisms and of plant genetics in general is proceeding at least as fast as our knowledge of human genetics. This is leading to a year-on-year increase in the possibilities for crop GM, which is coupled with increasing sophistication in GM methodology and a growing range of plant species for which GM has been shown to be feasible. The availability of GM as a tool for the plant-breeder is thus increasing. With GM already established in agriculture in several countries, it is likely to achieve even greater penetration or widespread use over the next ten years. One's reaction to all this depends of course on the side one takes in the debate, but whatever one's view, the increasing application of GM intensifies the challenge of working for global justice in respect of its use.

In the UK, the data from the farm-scale trials have been analysed and the results were published at the end of 2003. Then will follow the government's decision on whether to allow the commercial growth of GM crops in this country. Whatever decision is made, some will be infuriated and some will be pleased and there will be Christians in both camps, each group claiming that its views are consistent with biblical teaching. In many respects the debate so far has been quite fierce; the challenge now is to conduct any further discussion with grace and Christian love towards those with whom we disagree.

Genetic testing

In Chapter 6 we discussed extensively the increasing range of genetic tests that are coming on stream for use in detecting genetically based illness. If the number of available tests today is around sixty what is it likely to be in a year's time, in ten years' time? There will undoubtedly be pressure from both the medical community and the general public for increasing availability of such tests, but the information they provide may be difficult to handle. Are we prepared and able to support someone who knows that they have a late-onset genetic condition, or to listen, non-judgmentally, to prospective parents as they agonize over whether a particular genetic diagnosis is a justification for termination of a pregnancy?

The application of tests to pre-implantation embryos created by *in vitro* fertilization presents particular problems. Couples who are at particular risk of passing on a genetic condition to their offspring are already offered the chance of pre-implantation genetic diagnosis, so that only embryos that are free from the condition are placed in the mother's womb. But just how far will we want to go? As we discuss below ('Genetic modification for therapy and enhancement'), there is some support for allowing prospective parents to select against non-pathological conditions: for instance, rejecting one eye colour in favour of another, or selecting one sex over the other. Sex selection of embryos is already permitted in cases where one of the sexes, usually the male, will inevitably suffer from a particular condition. However, in the UK, the public is not supportive of sex selection for social reasons, such as family balance, reflecting the guidelines under which the regulatory authority, the HFEA, operates. But with writers such as Harris in the UK and Stock in the USA (see below) advocating a much freer approach to genetic selection of embryos, we wonder how long this prohibition will last.

One area in which current guidelines are certainly under pressure is the selection of embryos as potential stem-cell donors for pre-existing siblings. In summary, the HFEA allows such selection for genetic conditions: it allows selection of embryos in which the genetic lesion is absent and which are a tissue match for the older sibling. Until recently it did not allow tissue-matching alone (where the older sibling's condition, serious though it might be, does not have a directly genetic cause). We outlined the HFEA's reasoning behind this distinction in Chapter 6, but it needs to be said that, for some commentators and certainly for families involved, the distinction is very fuzzy. It seems very likely that, in addition to increasing numbers of cases for genetic selection plus tissue match, there will be increasing pressure to allow selection for tissue match alone. Indeed, the HFEA has responded to this pressure and is likely to allow such selection in the future. We want to assert again that there can be no biblical justification for using embryos in a consumerist way, but nevertheless the debate about the necessity for absolute protection of the embryo from fertilization onwards, set against the obligation to prevent and relieve suffering, will continue.

Genetic data
When shopping in Melbourne a few years ago, one of us was both impressed and slightly alarmed to see, as the machine read his credit card, that it printed out not only his name but his address at the other end of the world. Computer-accessible databases are capable of storing vast amounts of information about each of us; that is as true of genetic information as it is about credit-card details. We have noted that genetic information about people has the potential to be used to discriminate against individuals in areas such as employment and education. As the amount of genetic information potentially available about each one of us increases, so the scope for misuse increases. Some commentators have spoken of 'bar-code babies', suggesting that the information about an individual gathered by an automated set of genetic tests could be stored electronically, available for printing out and translation, rather as a bar-code reader at the supermarket checkout translates the pattern of bars into a price. At present this may seem a little far-fetched, but techniques are available for the simultaneous assay of many genes and it will not be long before these techniques are routinely applicable to genetic variation. Whether or not these techniques will have widespread application to humans to give individual bar-codes is another matter. Nevertheless, in our view regulations about the acquisition and storage of and access to genetic information

about individuals are essential, not only to ensure individual confidentiality but also to prevent misuse.

Genetic modification for therapy and enhancement

In Chapter 7 we discussed gene therapy – the replacement of malfunctioning genes by 'healthy' genes – and noted that it is restricted in law to somatic therapy: that is, any genetic change that is effected in the patient is not passed on to successive generations. However, this restriction is certainly under pressure and there are some, practitioners and commentators alike, who believe that germline gene therapy[3] should be permitted. Although the situations in which germline therapy might be regarded as necessary will be very rare, there is already enough interest to motivate active research with laboratory animals.

We also noted in Chapter 7 that the distinction between therapy and enhancement is blurred and thus there are some who believe that if germline gene therapy is permitted it will sooner or later lead to germline genetic enhancement. Further, some would welcome such developments. For example, Gregory Stock, the Director of the Programme on Medicine, Technology and Society at the UCLA School of Medicine, has recently developed such arguments in his book *Redesigning Humans – Choosing our Children's Genes* (Stock, 2002) and in a number of articles (e.g. Stock, 2003). He suggests that the question is simple: 'If we could make our baby brighter, or healthier, or more attractive, or ... otherwise gifted, or simply keep him or her from being overweight, why wouldn't we?' These ideas are very similar to the views of the philosopher John Harris, quoted in Chapter 7. However, Stock goes further in laying out a road map to widespread acceptance of genetic enhancement:

> Once it is appreciated that enhancement technology ... will be more useful in diminishing the cruelties and disappointments of life's genetic lottery than in improving upon its luckiest outcomes, the technology may seem far less threatening ... Affluent 'early users' may seek solely to benefit themselves and their children, but they will inadvertently serve as test pilots for humanity as a whole.

---

3. In germline gene therapy the properly functioning genes *will* be passed on from generation to generation.

Germline gene therapy is thus followed by 'therapeutic' enhancement, which is succeeded by a more general availability of enhancement.

On the questions of safety and variability of results that we discussed in Chapter 7, he is somewhat cavalier. Those 'test pilots' will check out the risks for those who are to follow: 'reproductive technologies are not like nuclear weapons. *Mistakes may bring problems to particular individuals and families* but cannot vaporise millions of innocent bystanders' (italics added). Thus he sees a society in which the option of genetic modification via *in vitro* fertilization is widely available and he suggests that its use should be regulated by market forces rather than by law. Leaving aside the difficulty of IVF becoming a high-throughput methodology, Stock's view of technology is very confident, very modernist, but the ethical stance is, despite attempts to suggest altruism, very postmodern: ethics is a matter of individual choice.

There is of course one sense in which these aims are laudable: they are at least partly motivated by the prevention of human suffering. An obvious danger, however, is that the weak and vulnerable become less and less valued. Their very existence becomes undesirable; once that happens, history shows what terrible things follow. There is an urgent need to put greatly increased resources into the care of those who are weak and vulnerable. They too are made in the image of God.

Cloning

During the preparation of this book there was one rather bizarre report of the birth of a cloned baby, plus two claims that pregnancies had been established with cloned embryos (see Chapter 8), followed more recently by several other claims. None of these claims of the birth of a clone could be confirmed, because the sect that made the claim refused to allow the babies' DNA to be tested. The other two claims, however, came from laboratories with experience in reproductive technologies and were not so lightly dismissed. Nevertheless, both these laboratories have yet to demonstrate the actual birth of a cloned baby. Whatever the reality of these claims, there is clearly an interest, albeit somewhat sinister, in the possibility of producing a human clone. This is despite statements from developmental biologists that cloning primates presents particular problems that are not seen with other mammals. Notwithstanding these particular difficulties with primates, there are some scientists who wish to proceed with human cloning. For example, Panayiotis Zavos, a fertility expert in the Kentucky Center for Reproductive Medicine, offered to use cloning technology in order that journalist Silvia Grilli could have a baby (see Grilli, 2003). She was offered the procedure at a cost of $50,000 and, because cloning is illegal in the USA (as in the UK), the insertion of the cloned embryo into her uterus would need to be done in, for instance, Ukraine or Lebanon (where there are no laws forbidding cloning). As in the purchase of genetic enhancement, we note the power of money, together with a modernist confidence in the power of the technology but a postmodern take on ethics: every position is as valid as any other; if individuals want to pay to be cloned then why should they be prevented?

Post-human?

Although there are vocal protagonists for the adoption of genetic enhancement and cloning there are also voices urging caution. The members of the team that cloned Dolly, for example, have made it very clear that they regard cloning of humans as unethical (see Griffin, 2002). On a broader front, the philosopher and economic historian Francis Fukuyama believes that to apply these technologies to humans is to go down a very dangerous road. He suggests (Fukuyama, 2002: 101) that, if modification of humans becomes routine or even commonplace, thus putting human development very much in our own hands, we will lose our sense of what it is to be human: our human essence.

> And what is that human essence that we might be in danger of losing? For a religious person it might have to do with the divine gift or spark that all human beings are born with. From a secular perspective, it would have to do with human nature: the species-typical characteristics shared by all human beings *qua* human beings. That is ultimately what is at stake in the biotech revolution.

He goes on to suggest that if we can so obviously manipulate the development of individual humans, then we are in danger of ceasing to regard individual humans as special. This in turn will have social and political implications in terms of our understanding of human rights and of the possibility of political interference in the use of the technology. He thus argues that the road of human genetic enhancement and cloning leads to a 'post-human future'. It may be, as we noted in respect of Stock's positive acceptance of these technologies, that Fukuyama has under-estimated the difficulties of applying them *en masse*. Nevertheless, his contribution to the debate, arguing lucidly from a secular stance, is very thought-provoking.[4]

Onward, Christians, boldly?

We now return to a theme that we introduced in Chapter 2 and which has appeared from time to time through the rest of the book. How do we develop a Christian response to current and probable future developments in biological and biomedical science? The lack of direct, specific guidance in the Bible is a major difficulty and we must not make the error of trying to extract scientific statements from the Scriptures: the Bible is not a scientific textbook. Nevertheless, there are clear general principles for people's behaviour as individuals and communities and we need to seek wisdom in applying these principles to these current issues. Thus Richard Hays (1996: 6) writes (italics original):

> The use of the New Testament in normative ethics requires *an integrative act of the imagination*, a discernment about how our lives, despite their historical dissimilarity to the lives narrated in the New Testament, might fitly answer to that narration and participate in the truth that it tells ... *whenever we appeal to the authority of the New Testament, we are necessarily involved in metaphor-making, placing our community's life imaginatively within the world articulated by the texts.*

John Stott, as we noted before, puts it more straightforwardly in urging us to practise 'double listening': listening to our culture and listening to Scripture (Stott, 1992: 94).

Even with a considered and prayerful approach (see Chapter 2), however, it is almost inevitable that different Christians will come to different conclusions on particular matters. This should not cause us to refrain from engaging with the issues. Authentic Christian living

4. Incidentally, in his book *Our Post-human Future*, Fukuyama presents a brief but interesting analysis, from a secular standpoint, of religious views on human genetics in the USA (Fukuyama, 2002: 88–91).

includes both applying our Christianity to real situations and accepting one another where we are. Thus the American theologian Cole-Turner, speaking in the context of human cloning, states his belief that engagement with the issues of the day is a vital part of the witness of a living church (see Chapman, 1999: 122). As for different Christians reaching different conclusions, he suggests that theological silence on these questions is far worse than theological disagreement. In our experience, the very fact that Christians engage with the issues causes others to think about what they are doing and consider how it may be best used. Furthermore, what damages the cause of Christ is not that there are disagreements among Christians about these dilemmas. Rather, damage is caused when Christians disagree stridently, with hostility towards each other and with accusations about the Christian commitment of the other side. One of the hallmarks of Christians is that, even though they may differ over some issues, they love and serve one another: 'How good and pleasant it is when brothers[5] live together in unity' (Ps. 133:1).

Postscript

When the first draft of the human genome sequence was announced, Bill Clinton, the President of the USA at that time, said (among other things) that the knowledge would be used to improve both the quality and the length of human life. Indeed, he spoke of it becoming commonplace, even in the next generation, to live to at least a hundred years. This statement comes from a very Western position. In several of the world's poorest countries, mainly in Africa, average life expectancy is nearer forty years than eighty. Globally, there is a fundamental question about where the healthy, affluent West should concentrate its resources: on making its inhabitants ever more affluent and healthy, rather than improving the plight of those who daily contend with poverty, hunger and disease?

There is, however, another angle on this, highlighted in comments in media interviews with the Chicago scientist Richard Seed (Seed, 1999). By cloning himself, he says, he will have achieved immortality. Never mind that we all understand, even if he apparently does

---

5. And of course sisters!

not, that his actual self – who he is – would not be copied in a genetic clone, there is the underlying theme that we can now cheat death, or, as in Bill Clinton's comment, at least postpone it.

Thereby we are in danger of forgetting eternal perspectives, as has been so ably pointed out by theologian Robert Song (2002) and by biologist Michael Reiss[6] (Reiss, 2003). We are made for an existence with God; Jesus Christ, through his incarnation, death and resurrection, has re-opened the door to that existence. That life extends beyond death to a life where God will wipe every tear from our eyes. Death will be no more; mourning and crying and pain will be no more, for the former things will pass away (Rev. 21:4). That prospect, of course, is not a licence to ignore human suffering in this present life. The Christ who has opened for us the gate of eternal life is also the Christ who healed the sick, fed the hungry and comforted the bereaved. He requires us to do likewise. This takes us back to the challenge of modern bioscience and technology. It has a huge potential for good and also for harm. We have to work out how it may be used for the former while eschewing the latter. Therefore our prayer is:

> Lord, be my vision,
> Supreme in my heart,
> Bid every rival give way and depart;
> You my best thought
> In the day or the night,
> Waking or sleeping,
> Your presence my light.
>
> High King of heaven
> When battle is done,
> Grant heaven's joy to me,
> Bright heaven's sun:
> Christ of my own heart, whatever befall,
> Still be my vision, O Ruler of all.[7]

---

6. Reiss is also an ordained Christian minister.

7. English translation of an ancient Irish hymn; © The estate of Eleanor Hull, from *The Source*, selected and edited by E. Hull.

GLOSSARY

alleles   different versions of a gene; many genes can exist in two (and occasionally more) forms in the same position on a chromosome.

bacteriophage   a virus that infects bacteria.

blastocyst   the hollow ball of cells which is formed by the dividing cells of the fertilized egg before implantation.

carcinogen   a substance which can induce the formation of a cancer in the body.

chorionic villus sampling   examining cells from the edge of the placenta in order to make a prenatal diagnosis of a genetic disease.

chromosome   a long string of genes in the nucleus of a cell. The number of chromosomes is characteristic for an individual species: for example, the basal chromosome number in humans is twenty-three.

clone   an organism identical in genetic make-up to another, produced asexually from ancestor or stock.

consequentialism   an ethical system based on considering the likely outcome of a decision.

deontology   an ethical system based on absolute values, from which responsibilities and duties arise.

DNA   deoxyribonucleic acid, the chemical which carries genetic information.

double helix   the term used to describe the structure of DNA: the thread-like molecules which make up DNA are twisted round each other in a pair, forming a double helical structure. (A good example of a single helix is a 'spiral' staircase.)

eugenics   improving the (human) population by controlled breeding and/or selective sterilization in order to increase the number of people with 'desirable' characteristics and decrease those with characteristics regarded as 'undesirable'.

fallopian tubes   the tubes along which eggs (whether fertilized or not) pass into the uterus.

gamete   a reproductive cell, either sperm or egg, which contains half the number of chromosomes of the somatic cells of the body; at fertilization the gametes from the male (sperm) and female (egg or oocyte) unite to form the zygote, which therefore has two sets of genetic information, one from each parent.

gene   an individual hereditary unit in a chromosome, made up of a characteristic sequence of DNA.

gene flow   the spreading of genes between different varieties of organisms.

genome   the entire genetic make-up of an organism.

germ cells   (in multi-cellular animals) cells belonging to the line of cells which gives rise to **gametes**.

germ line   the cell lineages that give rise to the germ cells. In the context of genetic variation or genetic modification, variations or modifications that are inherited are said to be in the germ line.

haemophilia   an inherited disease in which the blood does not clot. The defective gene is carried by the female but the disease is present only in her sons: this is known as *X-linked recessive transmission*.

heterozygous   having dissimilar or alternative alleles (forms of a gene) for a given characteristic (contrast **homozygous**).

HFEA   the Human Fertilization and Embryology Authority, which regulates all artificial reproduction and research on embryos in the United Kingdom.

homozygous   having identical genes for a given characteristic (contrast **heterozygous**).

Human Genome Project   a multinational project which set out to map and sequence (i.e. determine the order of the genes' building-blocks) the entire gene set of human beings. The Project was started in 1990, building on extensive but uncoordinated previous work on human gene sequencing. By mid-2000 the sequences of about 85% of the genes had been determined; a 'final' version of an 'average' human genome sequence was presented in spring 2003.

implantation   the process by which the early embryo becomes attached to the lining of the uterus.

in vitro   literally 'in glass': that is, outside the body.

IVF   *in-vitro* fertilization: the fertilization of an egg with a sperm in the laboratory, outside the body.

lesion   Although the general usage implies a wound, biologists use the term to mean a specific malfunction. That malfunction may arise because of specific damage (a 'wound') at molecular level.

mammals 'warm-blooded' vertebrates which suckle their young.

modernism the reliance on science and technology as the basis for reason; having its origins in the eighteenth century.

mutation a genetic change occurring naturally which is passed on to subsequent offspring.

NGOs non-governmental organizations.

nucleus the cell 'compartment' that, in all organisms other than bacteria (which do not possess cell 'compartments'), contains the DNA.

oocyte literally, egg cell. Used by biologists as meaning the egg prior to fertilization. Medical usage may be more ambiguous: often refers to egg cells prior to release from the ovaries.

oncogenes genes which, when they are activated, cause cancer.

pantheism the belief that God indwells all natural things, making nature divine.

penetrance the frequency with which a gene shows an effect (i.e. the frequency of expression). If the gene always shows its effect, penetrance is said to be complete, or 100%. However, the effects of genes may be modified by other genes and/or by environmental factors, so that a particular allele does not always show its effects in the organism. If the sample size is large enough, the frequency of expression may be quantified and expressed as a percentage.

PGD pre-implantation genetic diagnosis: that is, the diagnosis of genetic disease in an *in vitro* embryo before implantation into the womb.

phenylketonuria a genetically caused metabolic disorder in which the body cannot utilize a common component of protein. This leads to a build-up of toxic byproducts and thus to damage to the nervous system and to mental incapacity. It is controlled by adherence to a very strict (and somewhat boring!) diet. Provided the diet is adhered to, people with this condition lead normal lives.

plasmids small extra pieces of DNA found in the cells of bacteria.

pluripotent a cell is pluripotent if it has the ability to develop into a limited range of cells; adult stem cells are pluripotent.

position effect variation in the effects of a gene incorporated into the genome of another organism, depending on its position.

postmodernism an umbrella term for a group of closely related philosophies that deny the possibility of knowing objective truth about anything (or, in some cases, that there is such a thing as objective truth). This has clear implications for science, which claims to investigate physical objective reality. There is no 'big story' or metanarrative that transcends our immediate view of the world (i.e. there is no room for a religion that involves a transcendent God). There are no absolutes. Religion, ethics and morals are all a matter of individual choice; thus postmodernism in general embraces relativism. Image and 'spin' matter more than substance.

precautionary principle the principle which states that measures should be taken to prevent harm without waiting to see whether or not a particular scientific development actually causes harm.

primates the highest order of mammals, which includes human beings.

primitive streak a strip of cells in the early embryo which appears about fourteen days after fertilization and becomes the nervous system.

promoter the on/off switch of a gene, which determines when it operates.

protein the basic building-blocks and 'working molecules' of cells; they are manufactured according to the information encoded in the genes (the code in a gene is a 'recipe' to build a particular protein).

stem cells the cells in the early embryo from which all the cells of the foetus will develop.

thalassaemia an inherited disease of the blood in which there is a major deficiency in the blood protein haemoglobin, causing a severe anaemia.

totipotent a cell is *totipotent* if it has the potential to develop into *any* of the cell types in the adult organism; this potential exists, for example, in embryonic stem cells.

transgenic carrying a gene from another variety or species.

vertebrates animals with a backbone, including mammals, birds, reptiles, amphibians and fishes.

REFERENCES

Alexander, D. (2001), *Rebuilding the Matrix*, Oxford: Lion Publishing.

American Society of Plant Biologists/Cook, R. J. (2002), 'Biotech crops, an environmental ally', *ASPB News*: May/June.

Baggott la Velle, L. (2002a), 'Starting human life: the new reproductive technologies', in J. Bryant, L. Baggott la Velle and J. Searle (eds), *Bioethics for Scientists*, 201–232, Chichester: John Wiley & Sons.

Baggott la Velle, L. (2002b), 'Animal experimentation in biomedical research', in J. Bryant, L. Baggott la Velle and J. Searle (eds), *Bioethics for Scientists*, 313–330, Chichester: John Wiley & Sons.

Barclay, O. R. (1992), 'Animal rights – a critique', *Science and Christian Belief* 4: 57–61.

Barnes, B. (2002), 'The public evaluation of science and technology', in J. Bryant, L. Baggott la Velle and J. Searle (eds), *Bioethics for Scientists*, 19–36, Chichester: John Wiley & Sons.

Beauchamp, T. L., and Childress, J. F. (1979), *Principles of Biomedical Ethics*, New York and Oxford: Oxford University Press.

Berry, A. C. (1993), *Beginnings: Christian Views of the Early Embryo*, London: Christian Medical Fellowship.

Berry, R. J. (ed.) (2000), *The Care of Creation: Focusing Concern and Action*, Leicester: IVP.

Bevan, M. (2002), 'Plant biology – the first harvest of crop genes', *Nature* 416: 390.

Bharathan, G., Chandrashekaran, S., May, T., and Bryant, J. (2002), 'Crop biotechnology and developing countries', in J. Bryant, L. Baggott la Velle and J. Searle (eds), *Bioethics for Scientists*, 171–198, Chichester: John Wiley & Sons.

Birkett, K. (1997), *Unnatural Enemies*, Sydney and London: Matthias Media.

Boguski, M. S. (2002), 'Comparative genomics: The mouse that roared', *Nature* 420: 515–516.

Bradley, A. (2002), 'Mining the mouse genome', *Nature* 420: 512–514.

Bruce, D. (2002a), 'Finding a balance over precaution', *Journal of Agricultural and Environmental Ethics* 15: 7–6.

Bruce, D. (2002b), 'A social contract for biotechnology – shared visions for risky technologies', *Journal of Agricultural and Environmental Ethics* 15: 279–285.

Bruce, D., and Horrocks, D. (eds) (2001), *Modifying Creation?*, Carlisle: Paternoster Publishing.

Bryant, J. A. (1976) *Molecular Aspects of Gene Expression in Plants*, London: Academic Press.

Bryant, J. A. (1992), 'Mapping the human genome: the human genome project', *Science and Christian Belief* 4: 105–125.

Bryant, J., and Baggott la Velle, L. (2003), 'A bioethics course for biology and science education students', *Journal of Biological Education* 37: 91–96.

Bryant, J., and Turnpenny, P. (2003), 'Genetic modification of animals and humans: principles, practice and possibilities', in C. Deane-Drummond (ed.), *Brave New World*, Edinburgh: T. & T. Clark, 5–26.

Bryant J., Baggott la Velle, L., and Searle, J. (eds) (2002), *Bioethics for Scientists*, Chichester: John Wiley & Sons.

Burley, J., and Harris, J. (1999), 'Human cloning and child welfare', *Journal of Medical Ethics* 25: 108–113.

Butler, D. (2002), 'Rice genome sequencers cook up merger', *Nature* 416: 573.

Butler, D., and Smaglik, P. (2000), 'Draft data leave geneticists with a mountain still to climb', *Nature* 405: 914–915.

Carson, D. A. (2002), 'Maintaining scientific and Christian truths in a postmodern world', *Science and Christian Belief* 14: 107–122.

Carson, R. (1962), *Silent Spring*, New York: Houghton Mifflin.

Chapman, A. R. (1999), *Unprecedented Choices*, Minneapolis, MN: Fortress.

Chapman, A. R. (2002), 'Patenting human genes: ethical and policy issues', in J. Bryant, L. Baggott la Velle and J. Searle (eds), *Bioethics for Scientists*, 265–278, Chichester: John Wiley & Sons.

Chomsky, N. (2000), *New Horizons in the Study of Language and Mind*, Cambridge: Cambridge University Press.

Christoforou, S. (2003), 'Seeds of change', *RSA Journal*, April: 24–25.

Cibelli, J. B., Kiessling, A. A., Cunniff, K., Richards, C., Lanza, R. P., and West, M. D. (2001), 'Somatic cell nuclear transfer in humans: pronuclear and early embryonic development', *Journal of Reproductive Medicine* 2: 25–31.

Clark, S. R. L. (1984), *The Moral Status of Animals*, Oxford: Oxford Paperbacks, Oxford University Press.

Clothier, C. (1991), *Report of the Committee on the Ethics of Gene Therapy* (Cm. 1788), London: Stationery Office Books.

Cole-Turner, R. (1993), *The New Genesis: Theology and the Genetic Revolution*, Louisville, KY: Westminster/John Knox Press.

Cole-Turner, R. (1995), 'Religion and gene patenting', *Science* 270: 52.

Cole-Turner, R. (1997), 'At the beginning', in R. Cole-Turner (ed.), *Human Cloning: Religious Responses*, Louisville, KY: Westminster/John Knox Press.

Collins, F. (1999a), 'The human genome project: tool of atheistic reductionism or embodiment of Christian mandate to heal?' *Science and Christian Belief* 11: 99–111.

Collins, F. (1999b), 'Medical and societal consequences of the human genome project', *The New England Journal of Medicine* 341: 28–37.

Collins, F. S. (2002), 'Human genetics', in J. F. Kilner, C. C. Hook and D. B. Uustal (eds), *Cutting Edge Bioethics: A Christian Exploration of Technologies and Trends*, 3–17, Grand Rapids, MI, and Cambridge: William B. Eerdmans.

Conway, G. (1997), *The Doubly Green Revolution*, London: Penguin Books.

Conway, G. (2000), 'Crop biotechnology: benefits, risks and ownership', *OECD Conference: The Scientific and Health Aspects of Genetically Modified Foods*, 28 February–1 March 2000, Edinburgh.

Cook, D. (1996), *Blind Alley Beliefs*, 2nd ed., Leicester: IVP.

Cook, D. (2002), *Question Time*, Leicester: IVP.

Crawley, M. J., Brown, S. L., Hails, R. S., Kohn, D., and Rees, M. (2001), 'Transgenic crops in natural habitats', *Nature* 409: 682–683.

Crawley, M. J., Hails, R. S., Rees, M., Kohn, D., and Buxton, J. (1993), 'Ecology of transgenic oilseed rape in natural habitats', *Nature* 363: 620–623.

Daniels, N. (1994), 'The genome project: individual differences and just health care', in T. F. Murphy and M. A. Lappé (eds), *Justice and the Human Genome Project*, 110–132, Berkeley, CA: University of California Press.

Dawkins, R. (1989), *The Selfish Gene*, 2nd ed., Oxford: Oxford University Press.

Dawkins, R. (1993), 'Don't panic; take comfort, it's not all in the genes', *Daily Telegraph*, 17 July.

Dawkins, R. (1995), *River Out of Eden*, London: Phoenix.

Dawkins, R. (1999), *The Extended Phenotype*, Oxford: Oxford University Press.

Dawkins, R. (2003), *A Devil's Chaplain*, London: Weidenfeld & Nicholson.

Deane-Drummond, C. (2000), *Creation through Wisdom: Theology and the New Biology*, Edinburgh: T. & T. Clark.

Deane-Drummond, C. E. (2001), *Biology and Theology Today*, London: SCM.

Deane-Drummond, C. (2003), 'How might a virtue ethic frame debates in human genetics?' in C. Deane-Drummond (ed.), *Brave New World*, Edinburgh: T. & T. Clark.

Dennett, D. C. (1995), *Darwin's Dangerous Idea*, New York: Simon & Schuster; London: Penguin Books.

Dennett, D. C. (2003), *Freedom Evolves*, New York: Viking; London: Allen & Unwin.

Doolittle, R. F. (2002), 'The parasite genome – the grand assault', *Nature* 419: 493–494.

Draper, H. (1994), 'Ethical theory applied to anaesthesia and intensive care', in W. E. Scott, M. D. Vickers and H. Draper (eds), *Ethical Issues in Anaesthesia*, 3–16, Oxford: Butterworth-Heinemann.

Dziobon, S. (1999), 'Germ-line gene therapy: is the existing UK norm ethically valid?' in A. K. Thompson and R. F. Chadwick (eds), *Genetic Information: Acquisition, Access and Control*, 255–265, New York: Kluwer Academic/Plenum.

European Ecumenical Commission for Church and Society (1996), *Critique of the Draft EC Patenting Directive*, Strasbourg: EECCS.

Finlay, G. (2003), '*Homo divinus*: The ape that bears God's image', *Science and Christian Belief* 15: 17–40.

Forster, R., and Marston, P. (1999), *Reason, Science and Faith*, Crowborough: Monarch Books.

Frey, R. G. (2002), 'Human use of non-human animals: a philosopher's perspective', in J. Bryant, L. Baggott la Velle and J. Searle (eds), *Bioethics for Scientists*, 265–278, Chichester: John Wiley & Sons.

Fukuyama, F. (2002), *Our Post-human Future*, New York: Farrar, Strauss & Giroux; London: Profile Books.

George, F. C. (2001), 'The need for bioethical vision', in J. F. Kilner, C. C. Hook and D. B. Ustal (eds), *Cutting Edge Bioethics: A Christian Exploration of Technologies and Trends*, Grand Rapids, MI, and Cambridge: William B. Eerdmans.

Gill, R. (1992) *Moral Communities: The 1992 Bishop John Prideaux Lectures*, Exeter: Exeter University Press.

Gore, M. E. (2003), 'Adverse effects of gene therapy: gene therapy can cause leukaemia – no shock, mild horror but a probe', *Gene Therapy* 10: 4.

Griffin, H. (2002), 'Cloning of animals and humans', in J. Bryant, L. Baggott la Velle and J. Searle (eds), *Bioethics for Scientists*, 279–296, Chichester: John Wiley & Sons.

Grilli, S. (2003), 'I went to the States to be cloned', *Guardian* G2, 27 February: 12–13.

Hails, R. S. (2000), 'Genetically modified plants – the debate continues', *Trends in Ecology and Evolution* 15: 14–18.

Harris, J. (1997), 'Is cloning an attack on human dignity?' *Nature* 387: 754.

Harris, J. (1998), *Clones, Genes and Immortality*, Oxford: Oxford University Press.

Hays, R. B. (1996), *The Moral Vision of the New Testament*, Edinburgh: T. & T. Clark.

Huang, J., Rozelle, S., Pray, C., and Wang, Q. (2002), 'Plant biotechnology in China', *Science* 295: 674–677.

Hughes, S. (2002), 'The patenting of genes for agricultural biotechnology', in J. Bryant, L. Baggott la Velle and J. Searle (eds), *Bioethics for Scientists*, 153–170, Chichester: John Wiley & Sons.

Hughes, S., and Bryant, J. (2002), 'GM crops and food: a scientific perspective', in J. Bryant, L. Baggott la Velle and J. Searle (eds), *Bioethics for Scientists*, 115–140, Chichester: John Wiley & Sons.

Hwang, W. S., Ryn, Y. J., Park, J. H., Park, E. S., Lee, E. G., Koo, J. M., Chun, H. Y., Lee, B. C., Kang, S. K., Kim, S. J., Ahn, C., Hwang, J. H., Park, K. Y., Cibelli, J. B., and Moon, S. Y. (2004), 'Evidence of a pluripotent human embryonic cell line derived from a cloned blastocyst', *Science* 303: article published on line on 12 February 2004: <www.sciencemag.org/cgi/content/abstract/1094515>.

Jeungst E. T. (1997), 'Can enhancement be distinguished from prevention in genetic medicine?' *Journal of Medicine and Philosophy* 22: 125–142.

John Paul II, Pope (1995), *Evangelium Vitae*, Encyclical Letter.

Jones D. G. (1984), *Brave New People*, Leicester: IVP.

Jones, D. G. (2002), 'Human cloning: a watershed for science and ethics?' *Science and Christian Belief* 14: 159–180.

Jones, S. (1996), *In the Blood: God, Genes and Destiny*, London: HarperCollins.

Jonsen, A. R. (1998), *The Birth of Bioethics*, Oxford: Oxford University Press.

Kass, L. (1998), 'The Wisdom of Repugnance', *New Republic* 2: 5–12.

Knoppers, B. M. (2000), 'Population genetics and benefit sharing', *Community Genetics* 3: 212–214.

Kolata, G. (1997), *Clone: The Road to Dolly and the Path Ahead*, London: Penguin Books; New York: William Morrow.

Kuhse, H. (1999), 'Preventing genetic impairments: does it discriminate against people with disabilities?' in A. K. Thompson and R. F. Chadwick (eds), *Genetic Information: Acquisition, Access and Control*, 17–30, New York: Kluwer Academic/Plenum.

Kuhse, H., and Singer, P. (eds) (1999), *Bioethics: An Anthology*, Oxford: Blackwell.

Leopold, A. (1949), *A Sand County Almanac*, Oxford: Oxford University Press.

Linzey, A. (1987), *Christianity and the Rights of Animals*, London: SPCK.

Linzey, A. (1993) 'Animal rights: a reply to Barclay', *Science and Christian Belief* 5: 47–51.

McCarthy, B. (1997), *Faith and Fertility*, Leicester: IVP.

McCreath, K. J., Howcroft, J., Campbell, K. H. S., Colman, A., Schnieke, A. E., and King, A. J. (2000), 'Production of gene-targeted sheep by nuclear transfer from cultured somatic cells', *Nature* 405: 1066–1069.

McGee, A. N. (1891), 'An experiment in human stirpiculture', *American Anthropologist* 4: 319–329.

McGrath, A. E. (1993), *Evangelism and the Future of Christianity*, London: Hodder & Stoughton.

McGrath, A. E., and Wenham, D. (1993), 'Evangelicalism and biblical authority', in A. E. McGrath and A. T. France (eds), *Evangelical Anglicans*, 22–36, London: SPCK.

MacIntyre, A. (1981), *After Virtue*, Notre Dame, IN: University of Notre Dame Press.

Marshall, E. (2000), 'Human genome: rival sequencers celebrate a milestone together', *Science* 288: 2294–2295.

Marteau, T., and Richards, M. (eds) (1996), *The Troubled Helix*, Cambridge: Cambridge University Press.

Messer, N. (2001), 'Human genetics and the image of the triune God', *Science and Christian Belief* 13: 99–111.

Messer, N. G. (2003), 'The Human Genome Project: health and the tyranny of normality', in C. Deane-Drummond (ed.), *Brave New World*, Edinburgh: T. & T. Clark, 91–115.

Meyer, S. (2002), 'Questioning GM foods', in J. Bryant, L. Baggott la Velle and J. Searle (eds), *Bioethics for Scientists*, 141–152, Chichester: John Wiley & Sons.

Midgley, M. (2000), 'Biotechnology and monstrosity – Why we should pay attention to the "yuk factor"', *Hastings Centre Reports* 30: 7–15.

Moore, P. (2001) *Babel's Shadow: Genetic Technologies in a Fracturing Society*, Oxford: Lion Publishing.

Moreno, J. D. (1991), 'Ethics consultation as moral engagement', *Bioethics* 5: 44–56.

Murray, D. R. (2003), *Seeds of Concern*, Sydney: University of New South Wales Press; Wallingford: CABI.

Nuffield Council on Bioethics (1999), *Genetically Modified Crops: the Ethical and Social Issues*, London: Nuffield Council on Bioethics.

Nuffield Council on Bioethics (2002a), *The Ethics of Patenting DNA*, London: Nuffield Council on Bioethics.

Nuffield Council on Bioethics (2002b), *Genetics and Human Behaviour: The Ethical Context*, London: Nuffield Council on Bioethics.

O'Donovan, O. (1984), *Begotten or Made?* Oxford: Oxford University Press.

Oppenheimer, S. (2003), *Out of Eden: The Peopling of the World*, London: Constable.

Packer. J. I. (1993), *God Has Spoken*, London: Hodder & Stoughton.

Paul, D. B. (1998), *Controlling Human Heredity, 1865 to the Present*, Amhurst, NY: Humanity Press.

Pederson, R. (1999), 'Embryonic stem cells for medicine', *Scientific American*, April: 45–49.

Perry, J. N. (2003), 'Genetically modified crops', *Science and Christian Belief* 15: 141–163.

Peterson, J. C. (2001), *Genetic Turning Points: The Ethics of Human Genetic Intervention*, Grand Rapids, MI: William B. Eerdmans.

Pinker, S. (2000), *The Language Instinct: How the Mind Creates Language*, 2nd ed., New York: Harper Row/Perennial Books.

Polkinghorne, J. (1998), *Science and Theology – An Introduction*, London: SPCK; Minneapolis, MN: Fortress.

Pomerai, D. de (2002), 'Human use of non-human animals: a biologist's view', in J. Bryant, L. Baggott la Velle and J. Searle (eds), *Bioethics for Scientists*, 265–278, Chichester: John Wiley & Sons.

Potter, V. R. (1971), *Bioethics: Bridge to the Future*, Englewood Cliffs, NJ: Prentice Hall.

Rechsteiner, M. C. (1991), 'The Human Genome Project: misguided science policy', *Trends in Biochemical Sciences* 16: 455.

Reed, E. D. (2003), 'Property rights, genes and heredity', in C. Deane-Drummond (ed.), *Brave New World*, Edinburgh: T. & T. Clark.

Reeve, C. (2002), interviewed by Oliver Burkeman: interview published as 'Man of steel', *Guardian* G2, 17 September: 1–4.

Regan, T. (1983), *The Case for Animal Rights*, London: Routledge.

Reiss, M. (2002), 'Introduction to ethics and bioethics', in J. Bryant,
    L. Baggott la Velle and J. Searle (eds), *Bioethics for Scientists*, 3–17,
    Chichester: John Wiley & Sons.
Reiss, M. J. (2003), 'And in the world to come, life everlasting', in C. Deane-
    Drummond (ed.), *Brave New World*, Edinburgh: T. & T. Clark, 44–67.
Ridley, M. (1994), *The Red Queen: Sex and the Evolution of Human Nature*,
    London: Penguin Books.
Ridley, M. (1997), *The Origins of Virtue*, London: Penguin Books.
Ridley, M. (2001), 'Technology and the environment: the case for optimism'.
    The Prince Philip Lecture, Royal Society of Arts, London.
Ridley, M. (2003a), *Nature via Nurture*, London: Fourth Estate.
Ridley, M. (2003b), 'We've never had it so good – and it's all thanks to
    science', *Guardian Life*, 4 April: 8–9.
Robinson, D. (1999), *Nietzsche and Postmodernism*, New York: Totem Books;
    Cambridge: Icon Books.
Rolston, H. (1999), *Genes, Genesis and God*, Cambridge: Cambridge
    University Press.
Rorty, R. (1979), *Philosophy and the Mirror of Nature*, Princeton, NJ:
    Princeton University Press.
Rose, S. (1997), *Lifelines: Biology, Freedom, Determinism*, London: Penguin
    Books.
Rose, S. (2003), 'Natural conclusion', *Guardian Review*, 19 April: 13.
Scott, P. (2003), 'Is the goodness of God good enough? The human genome
    project in theologico-political perspective', in C. Deane-Drummond (ed.),
    Brave New World, Edinburgh: T. & T. Clark, 294–318.
Seed, R. (1999), 'You and I are obsolete', *CORE conference on Being Human:
    The Science and Philosophy of Cloning*, London, 30 March.
Shakespeare, T. (1998), 'Choices and rights: eugenics, genetics and disability
    equality', *Disability and Society* 13: 665–682.
Shapiro, R. (1991), *The Human Blueprint: The Race to Unlock the Secrets of
    Our Genetic Script*, New York: St Martin's Press.
Simms, A. (1999), *Selling Suicide*, London: Christian Aid.
Singer, P. (1986), *Animal Liberation: A New Ethic for our Treatment of
    Animals*, London: Jonathan Cape.
Singer, P. (1994), *Rethinking Life and Death*, Oxford: Oxford University
    Press.
Smaglik, P. (2000a), 'Clinical trials end at gene-therapy institute', *Nature* 405:
    497.
Smaglik, P. (2000b), 'Relations thaw between genome rivals as finish line
    draws near', *Nature* 405: 721.
Snowden, R., and Snowden, E. (1993), *The Gift of a Child: A Guide to Donor
    Insemination*, Exeter: University of Exeter Press.
Song, R. (2002), *Human Genetics*, London: Darton, Longman & Todd.
Stock, G. (2002), *Redesigning Humans: Choosing our Children's Genes*,
    London: Profile Books.
Stock, G. (2003), 'Unnatural birth', *RSA Journal*, April: 34–37.

Stott, J. R. W. (1986), *The Cross of Christ*, Leicester: IVP.

Stott, J. R. W. (1992), *The Contemporary Christian*, Leicester: IVP.

Stott, J. R. W. (1999), *New Issues Facing Christians Today*, Grand Rapids, MI: Zondervan.

Strachan, T., and Read, A. P. (1996), *Human Molecular Genetics*, Oxford: Bios Scientific.

Taylor, J. L. (2002), 'The postmodern attack on scientific realism', *Science and Christian Belief* 14: 99–106.

Taylor, P. (2002), *For What it is Worth*, London: CARE.

Teichman, J. (1996), *Social Ethics*, Oxford: Blackwell.

Temple, W. (1941), *Citizen and Churchman*, London: Eyre & Spottiswoode.

Thompson, S., Clarke, A. R., Pow, A. M., Hooper, M. L., and Melton, D. W. (1989), 'Germline transmission and expression of a corrected hrpt gene produced by gene targeting in embryonic stem cells', *Cell* 56: 313–321.

Trewavas, A. J. (2001), 'Urban myths about organic agriculture', *Nature* 410: 409–410.

Trigg, R. (2003), 'A Christian basis for science', *Science and Christian Belief* 15: 3–15.

Tudge, C. (1998), *Neanderthals, Bandits and Farmers – How Agriculture Really Began*, London: Weidenfield & Nicholson.

Turnpenny, P., and Bryant, J. (2002), 'Human genetics and genetic enhancement', in J. Bryant, L. Baggott la Velle and J. Searle (eds), *Bioethics for Scientists*, 241–264, Chichester: John Wiley & Sons.

Vogel, G. (2001), 'Infant monkey carries jellyfish gene', *Science* 291: 226.

Warnock, M. (1984), *Report of the Committee of Enquiry into Human Fertilisation and Embryology*, London: HMSO.

Warnock, M. (1998), *An Intelligent Person's Guide to Ethics*, London: Duckworth.

Wellcome Trust (1998), *Public Perspectives on Human Cloning: A Social Research Study*, London: Wellcome Trust.

White, L., Jr (1967), 'The historical roots of our ecologic crisis', *Science* 155: 1203–1207.

Wilkie, T. (1994), *Perilous Knowledge: The Human Genome Project and its Implications*, London: Faber & Faber.

Williams-Jones, B. (2002), 'History of a gene patent: tracing the development, marketing, and application of commercial BRCA testing in Canada', *Health Law Journal* 10: 121–144 (text available at <www.genethics.ca/personal/publications.html>).

Wilmut, I., Schnieke, A. E., McWhir, J., Kind, A. J., and Campbell, K. H. S. (1997), 'Viable offspring derived from fetal and adult mammalian cells', *Nature* 385: 810–813.

Wilson, E. O. (1978), *On Human Nature*, Cambridge, MA: Harvard University Press.

Wilson, E. O. (1998), 'The biological basis of morality', *The Atlantic Monthly* 281: 53–70.

Winston, R. (2003), *Walking with Cavemen*, BBC TV series.

Wirth, D. F. (2002), 'The parasite genome – biological revelations', *Nature* 419: 495–496.
Wright, R. T. (1989), *Biology Through the Eyes of Faith*, Leicester: Apollos.
Wyatt, J. (1998), *Matters of Life and Death*, Leicester: IVP.
Wyatt, J. (2003), 'Send in the clones?' *Third Way* 26: 23–25.